MANAGEMENT
BY
PARTICIPATION

MANAGEMENT

BY

PARTICIPATION

Creating a Climate for Personal and Organizational Development

ALFRED J. MARROW, Ph.D.

DAVID G. BOWERS, Ph.D.

STANLEY E. SEASHORE, Ph.D.

HARPER & ROW, PUBLISHERS

NEW YORK, EVANSTON, AND LONDON

Contents

PART III

The Outcome: Weldon, 1964

Contributors

Charles Brooks
    Geoffrey Ladhams Associates, training engineers and consultants

Gilbert David, Ph.D.
    Leadership Development Associates, consulting psychologists

Hyman Kornbluh
    Director, Labor Education and Service Division of the Institute of Labor and Industrial Relations, the University of Michigan

Seymour A. Marrow
    President, Harwood Manufacturing Corporation

John R. Nelson
    Vice President for Manufacturing, Harwood Manufacturing Corporation

Robert F. Pearse, Ph.D.
    Professor of Behavioral Sciences, Boston University

Ernest E. Roberts
    President, Norris & Elliott, Inc., consulting engineers

John F. Smith
    Plant Manager, Weldon Manufacturing Company

Acknowledgments

The work reported in this book was supported financially by the Harwood Manufacturing Corporation and, in part, by the Survey Research Center of the Institute for Social Research at the University of Michigan. We are grateful for the interest and counsel of our colleagues: Rensis Likert, John R. P. French, Jr., Arnold Tannenbaum, and Robert L. Kahn. Miss Ofelia Rodriguez was responsible for the research data analysis, and helped substantially with the organization of this report. Mrs. Beatrice Pelzer gave invaluable assistance in the preparation of the manuscript.

Foreword

This volume reports an extraordinarily successful improvement of a failing organization through the introduction of a new management system. An unprofitable enterprise was made profitable, and a better place to work, in the short span of two years. Many managers and students of management will want to know how this was done.

The maturing of the social and behavioral sciences has brought them to a more active role in management. Research scientists and their professional colleagues have become more involved in the central, as well as the peripheral, problems of organizations. It is valuable to have another detailed account of the ways in which sociologists and psychologists may contribute to the choice of goals and strategies in management, and to the realization of those goals.

A significant feature of this process is the necessity for integrated work among the specialists in various management disciplines—accountants, engineers, general managers, and behavioral specialists. The necessity of using a systems approach in managing an organization and in efforts to introduce change becomes evident as the Weldon story unfolds. Changes in all major factors such as the management system, the technology and engineering, leadership training, communications, decision-making, compensation, earnings, and union-management relations were undertaken in a planned, coordinated manner and in an orderly sequence. The result was an integrated whole consisting of compatible parts. The trends in the improvements obtained reflect the value of the interaction and mutual reinforcement of all the changes made. For example, the engineering and job changes would not have yielded such large improvement had there not been cooperative motivation among supervisors and operators. This motivation was created by changes in the management system and leadership styles. Similarly, the sensitivity training of supervisory and managerial personnel was completely compatible with the new management philosophy and the other changes being introduced. The re-engineering of the work and the improved organization and definition of jobs around which problem-solving could be done added to the effectiveness of the training in problem-solving.

The candor with which the successes and failures are described adds to the value of this volume. All too often the failures in an undertaking are buried, while the successes only are reported; yet frequently more can be learned from the efforts that have failed; so it is refreshing to be given the whole picture.

Academic tradition prescribes a dispassionate, objective view of ideas. This report, however, in spite of its charts and tables and in spite of the candidly evaluative chapter by the team of observers, is fundamentally a partisan book. While dealing with some of the difficulties in applying a participative approach to management, it describes events carried out with conviction as well as with a theory. It is written about and by people caught up in the press of events and in the enthusiasm of applying ideas in which they believe. Many readers will appreciate the importance both of enthusiasm in getting a program into action, and of evaluating the ideas on their own merit on grounds of common sense, rationality, and scientific evidence.

The need for measurement through a span of time is demonstrated by the Weldon experience. The periodic measurements of all the complex processes of this industrial organization enabled all those engaged in the changes to appraise, periodically, the success of their efforts and to modify them as necessary. Measurements also revealed the consequences through time of changes in such factors as the methods of doing the work, the nature of each job, the organizational structure, the role of managers and supervisors, and the training provided in job instructions and in leadership interaction processes. In addition to being valuable to the Weldon project, these measurements add an important body of findings to aid our general knowledge about organizations.

This volume makes clear the contribution which quantitative social science research can make to an enterprise. General principles and specific insights emerging from such research were used to plan and guide all changes made in the Weldon plant. The report of this experience will prove to be of great value to anyone interested in improving the operations of a business or other kind of organization.

RENSIS LIKERT

DIRECTOR, INSTITUTE
FOR SOCIAL RESEARCH,
THE UNIVERSITY OF
MICHIGAN

Preface

This book is about people who are busy making a living. It is about those who manage and those who are managed, and about the everyday problems of working together in an organization. These people—whether they get along or quarrel, love the work or hate it—are constantly acting, reacting, and interacting, regardless of differences in titles, skills, and salaries.

People can enjoy working together far more than they do. For a majority, however, dissatisfaction, ill will, and conflict have produced anxiety, resentment, and hostility, with disruptive and harmful consequences for the individual and the organization. Until World War II little was done about the problem. Significant studies by behavioral scientists in recent years have provided practical insights into the "why" of the stresses that develop in the process of human interaction at work. Much of the research has focused on new methods for introducing changes to increase organizational effectiveness without creating distressing side effects.

This book is an account of what can happen when these methods are applied. It all started with what seemed to be a routine business acquisition. A middle-sized corporation in the apparel industry purchased a competitor manufacturing the same product. The initial purposes were greater efficiency, lower costs, and higher profits. A closer look at the two companies, however, revealed differences as well as similarities so striking as to make the combined enterprises a unique study in comparative management and organizational structure.

Only rarely in the history of the behavioral sciences have the conditions been so right and the circumstances so suitable for evaluating two contrasting managerial approaches. Perhaps even rarer were the opportunities: (1) carefully to set up in advance the design, measurement, and methods of data collection of a planned program of change; (2) to follow the process of attitude and behavior modifications; and (3) to measure the effect of the purposeful changes on attitudes, behavior, production, absenteeism, turnover, cost per unit, and—finally—net profit.

In important respects the two organizations were remarkably alike. When the Harwood Manufacturing Corporation took over its leading competitor, the Weldon Manufacturing Company each firm employed about 1,000 people; their plants were both about thirty years old; and both turned out the same product—pajamas. Both companies used the same raw materials, followed similar manufacturing processes on much the same machinery, and sold at competitive prices in similar and overlapping markets.

The merger thus appeared to be a thoroughly logical one, without apparent difficulty or particular problems. Moreover, in making the purchase, Harwood planned no major changes in Weldon's product, management, or manufacturing facilities. Weldon's entire staff was to be retained, and the company's two owner-managers, turned salaried managers, were to continue as before. Efficiencies were to be introduced wherever indicated, but the companies were to continue to operate separately and maintain separate identities.

Soon after the merger, however, it became apparent that the differences in leadership style and in managerial system between the two companies were so great as to make it impossible to carry out the original plan under which Weldon was to continue as an autonomous division of Harwood. Where Harwood emphasized and encouraged participative methods in meeting its problems, Weldon operated under the traditional authority-obedience system.

As a pioneer in the application of behavioral science to the problems of management, Harwood had some twenty-five years of history in seeking to improve its organizational effectiveness with participative methods. In asserting the effectiveness of their management approach, Harwood's executives could point not only to gratifying job satisfaction among their employees (and themselves) but also to the hard criteria of profits and productivity.

Weldon, on the other hand, with its authoritarian methods

and paramilitary system, was discovered by the new owners to be plagued by high costs, beset by low morale, and suffering from an inadequate return on investment. A study of the two companies confirmed the original impression that all other considerations were nearly equal and that the major cause of the contrasting performance of the two companies lay in their opposite management practices. Once the basic difference in approach to management of the organizations was recognized, the task became one of introducing organizational changes into the Weldon enterprise that would bring the Harwood management approach into play—and to do so quickly, smoothly, and with the least human and financial cost.

For help, the Harwood people called in the Survey Research Center of the University of Michigan's Institute for Social Research to measure, interpret, and analyze employee attitudes and behavior during the period of change. Members of the institute were also to observe the events that took place and record what was done and what happened.

A second team of behavioral scientists were brought in as "change agents" to design and carry out a program to increase managerial competence, improve interpersonal relations, train supervisors and executives in the principles of participative management, and serve as trainers in a development program for all members of the staff. Two groups of engineering consultants were employed to introduce needed technological improvements. The entire project was to be directed by the senior executives of the Harwood enterprise.

Thus the foundations were set for an unusual collaboration of practitioners, engineers, and behavioral scientists to introduce changes aimed at increasing efficiency, improving organizational effectiveness, and helping employees at every level to improve their performance on the job and their feelings of pleasure and accomplishment in their work.

While there have been a few studies which attempted to measure improvement in organizational effectiveness resulting from a planned change program, the findings have been far from conclusive. Systematic observation, controlled experimentation, reliable before-and-after data—all have been lacking.

Now, an additional study is in hand. We are able to present a detailed and well-documented report on what happened when the attitudes, behavior, values, and leadership style of an entire organization were systematically and purposefully changed.

Customarily, the report of such a change effort would be made from the single viewpoint of the engineering or management consultant, or that of an author summarizing the process for all involved. In this case, the participative approach extends to the manner and mode of presentation. It is a collaboration by those who shared the responsibilities for the change. Consequently, the following chapters were written by the people who created and implemented the program. They will depict the events and changes as they perceived them. They are best qualified to explain what happened. Since they also know the motivations and philosophy behind the decisions, they can provide valuable insights into the delicate process of changing attitudes, behavior, and values.

This book is written, first, for an alert and literate management, men who seek to broaden their understanding of the problems created by technical and social change, and who need to get some ideas about what one can do—concretely—about planned changes. It is hoped, too, that the book may offer behavioral scientists a useful example of the richly complex historical, technical, and economic setting within which purposeful social change in business organizations can be made to occur. It is for this reason that the book will contain living detail about specific events in the process of change—their time sequence and schedule, their initiation and their rationale, their difficulties of execution—and their ultimate outcome.

A.J.M.

PART I

THE WELDON COMPANY, 1962

Introduction

THE FIRST PART of this volume describes the history of the Weldon Manufacturing Company as it bears on our story, and describes the condition of the company in 1962 when the new owners undertook to rejuvenate its technology and to rebuild its human organization.

An initial chapter, by the president of Harwood, records his impressions and plans as they were formed during and after the purchase negotiation period, while he gradually became acquainted with Weldon. The second chapter, similar in purpose, gives the views of the Harwood vice president for manufacturing from the perspective of one primarily concerned with the Weldon plant and its people.

The Harwood company provided a model for the Weldon company during its change program, a standard against which progress could be assessed, and a source for guiding ideas with respect to organizational values, goals, strategies, and tactics. Chapter 3 sets forth the Harwood approach to management.

Further light on the condition of Weldon in 1962 might be found in the experience of the Weldon employees and their union—the Amalgamated Clothing Workers of America—in dealing with the former Weldon management. We asked an academic colleague, a former organizer for ACWA with personal knowledge of these events, to sketch their history. He not only called on his own recollections, but also reviewed the union's files and interviewed other union people who have been concerned with the Weldon case.

The final chapter in Part I is a comparison of the Weldon and Harwood companies, particularly of their manufacturing plants and organizations, from the perspective of a research scientist. This chapter includes "hard" figures on the performance of the two plants, along with information and observations relevant to understanding their organizational structures, their ways of working, and the values and feelings embodied in their organizational processes.

These chapters refer to Weldon as it was in mid-1962, several months after purchase by Harwood and at the time when it became clear that a change program would be needed to salvage the firm.

1

HARWOOD BUYS WELDON

Seymour A. Marrow*

ON JANUARY 1, 1962, when the Harwood Manufacturing Corporation became the owner of the Weldon company, months of negotiations were completed and months of revelation and adjustment began. The story concerns not only the elements of risk and uncertainty common to acquisitions, mergers, and business expansions, but also the universal process of organization change.

Initially, the possibilities for the sale and acquisition were seen by an officer of a bank where both companies maintained accounts. He brought the principals together and facilitated the negotiations in the bank's executive offices. Because the timing was so opportune, negotiations were concluded after only four months of investigation and formal meetings.

Harwood's motive was largely financial: It had underutilized capital, and the acquisition provided an opportunity for growth in its own industry by enlarging its market. Weldon could provide an established volume of sales of a nationally advertised brand of garments distributed in leading stores here and abroad. Harwood had been unable to sell its own brand in significant quantity to the higher-priced "quality" market to which Weldon sold in depth.

---

* President of the Harwood Manufacturing Corporation.

5

This promised a highly desirable balance. Weldon, as the leading brand house in the pajama industry, would complement Harwood's successful chain-store business. While Harwood concentrated on selling to large national distributors under their private brands, Weldon could expand its own brand-name sales to leading department stores and quality men's shops. Ownership of Weldon would enable Harwood to discontinue the costly efforts to establish its own higher-priced brand distribution.

With this in mind, our intention was to continue Weldon as an independent company rather than to unify the two organizations. Each company would have its own plants, separate sales organizations, and separate markets. Weldon's entire management would be retained, including the two owners. The emphasis would be on managerial continuity.

After acquisition, changes were to be limited to modernization of manufacturing facilities and improvement in work methods at the Weldon plant. Improved equipment and production systems were to be installed, modeled after those existing at other Harwood plants. Such changes would provide improved customer service, tighter quality control, and lower manufacturing costs. It was assumed that sales volume would at least be maintained, and that lowered costs from increased plant efficiency would permit adequate profits. However, for reasons that did not become clear until some months after acquisition—when serious weaknesses came to light—matters did not work out as intended.

Unsuspected weaknesses were gradually discovered in every area of Weldon's operation: merchandising, manufacturing, and internal operations. Harwood could not have discovered them before the purchase was made. Financial reports, without any distortion, may often fail to reveal serious problems; plant inspections and staff interviews during negotiation must be rather superficial; any seller must present the best picture of his enterprise; full disclosure could lead to serious disadvantages to the seller if the deal fell through, for a competitor would have obtained critical information. In addition, the Weldon management itself was not fully aware of the scope of

its difficulties. Thus, Harwood had to take the kinds of risk
which all mergers normally entail.

The Weldon Background

In the months following acquisition, a detailed picture of the
Weldon organization emerged, clarifying both its strengths
and its weaknesses. The history of Weldon proved to be reveal-
ing in our efforts to understand the conditions we found.

Early in the 1940s Weldon became one of the fastest-
growing producers of quality pajamas. As a result of wartime
scarcities, a sellers' market had developed. The Weldon partners obtained a preferential position with many fabric sup-
pliers and could count on generous allotments of good fabrics,
which they made up well and distributed judiciously. By the
end of World War II, Weldon had become one of the recognized and highly respected leaders in the industry. The partners built on this deserved reputation. By the mid-1950s,
Weldon was employing about 3,500 people in five plants.

But the company's growth, and the gradual change in market conditions, were not accompanied by any change in managerial practices. The company was run to the extent possible
—almost solely—by the two owners, who personally and with
considerable energy and competence made the necessary plans
and decisions. While the partners' personal role in every decision had contributed to the company's rise, it now began to
contribute to its decline. Instead of strengthening and broaden-
ing the managerial organization, the partners retained personal
control even when confronted by more numerous and more
complicated responsibilities.

One partner ran the merchandising side of the business
while the other ran the production side. Each partner directed
his own area independently of the other. Perhaps this was due
to differences in personality, social outlook, and interests, for
it seemed easier for them to keep apart even in the conduct of
their common business. The partner responsible for production
rarely participated in sales, advertising, or marketing decisions.
The partner responsible for merchandising rarely intruded in

manufacturing. Their contacts were limited to major decisions on policy, replacement of key executives, and similar episodic organizational problems.

While the managerial style of both partners was in the traditional authoritarian mold, personality differences were evident. The merchandising partner, who was outgoing, frequently would solicit ideas from his staff on policy formulation —but would always make the final decision to suit himself. When the merchandising partner did delegate authority it was poorly defined. Jurisdictions overlapped, and it was never clear who was free to make what decision and under what conditions. So little information was given to the staff that they could not handle ordinary recurring problems without asking for top-level help. The manufacturing partner, more taciturn and uncommunicative, was a typical one-man boss, rarely sharing problems, plans, or objectives. He would announce schedules, budgets, or production quotas, expect the staff to meet them, and give a difficult time to any who failed to do so.

The partners did not change their management methods. After all, their methods had brought them wealth and fame in the industry. Why change them? Besides, the methods they used were in vogue in an industry where companies were founded by individuals who started with little money and great ambitions. Management, for them, was mainly "do-it-yourself."

Weldon's history of growth coupled with insistence upon personal control by the partners led to failure of work relations among the managerial staff. Detailed rules developed to govern matters that could not be attended to personally by one of the partners. The authority and responsibilities of staff members became confining. Reports and records proliferated in ways suitable mainly for maintaining the control of the partners.

The rules and regulations developed partly in explicit form and partly by custom. For example, the type of transportation to be used on company trips was known, and adhered to on grounds of economy even at considerable wastage of managerial time and convenience. Allowances for sandwich costs when working overtime were set—and on a sliding scale according to salary. Commitment of small and obviously necessary expenditures for maintenance had to be approved personally by one of the partners, as a matter of procedure, without regard for the time loss and work delays involved.

Staff members were discouraged from making decisions on their own and from suggesting innovations. Higher-level managers were expected to—and did—intervene daily in the work of their subordinates, checking activities, passing judgment on routine matters, and often reversing unnecessarily actions taken under the press of events. Managers and supervisors at all levels became accustomed to this arrangement even though they were often frustrated by their inability to deal directly with matters well within their personal competence.

Such a system of control requires a reliable system for surveillance. Certain favored employees in different parts of the plant or office were encouraged to "report confidentially to the boss" any divergence from policies and procedures. Paperwork multiplied in response to work errors and in response to top management's need for detailed information. The reports, however, were not planned on any over-all basis for economy or to get information quickly to the operative levels of management. Some records were discovered to be deliberately falsified by people who feared the reactions of superiors; there occurred deliberate collusion in keeping important information from the partners.

Thus, the "controls" did not effectively control the activities of the organization, the rules did not regulate constructively, and the reports and records conveyed information of doubtful value to people who were in a poor position to react appropriately. All this meant heavy management cost, with little effective management obtained for it. Expenses mounted, profits declined, and no one could or would say why.

In this situation, extending over several years, the partners drove themselves almost to the point of collapse. They demanded the same of their staff. They spent evenings and week ends on the job and required all senior executives and many junior ones to do likewise. The situation gave rise to jealousy, intrigue, and bickering. A few of the more independent key executives left the organization, and became highly successful in new jobs.

The staff recognized the ability of the owners and, for this reason, did willingly cooperate. But they also were aware that management was not heeding its human responsibilities. The company had failed to set up a retirement plan, life insurance, employee health and hospital insurance, or any of the other voluntary fringe benefits which have become commonplace.

Two major Weldon ventures—which had puzzled the industry—were clarified in the light of the management picture disclosed after acquisition and in the light of their relationship to Weldon's decline. In 1953, Weldon had organized a new company to enter the lower-priced, mass production shirt and pajama business, despite Weldon's reputation as a manufacturer exclusively of higher-priced quality merchandise. This was surprising, as the low-priced market requires the most advanced technology, which Weldon was known to lack. In addition, Weldon undertook to make and sell women's pajamas, even though they are sold to different buyers and require styling and manufacturing different from men's pajamas; many wondered why Weldon entered this competitive and different market.

The answers to these puzzles became clear as we learned more of the Weldon history. The Weldon owners were ambitious, self-made, hard-driving men who made decisions without the protection of careful consultation with others. Significant in the ultimate failure of the shirt venture was their inability to delegate authority to or to consult with subordinates. As the company became more complex and dispersed over several plants, the workload accumulated and the owners continued personally to supervise every aspect of the operation. The problems overwhelmed the centralized system of management; chaos resulted. The shirt and low-priced pajama firm used up a considerable amount of working capital and was liquidated in 1956 after heavy losses. The experience weakened the or-

paid on a commission basis, promised impossibly fast deliveries at mutually conflicting dates. There was little provision for coordination or plant clearance.

Production schedules were set by the sales department. The recurrent conflicts in delivery promises forced them to demand almost daily changes in production priorities and frequently to demand partial deliveries. The effect in the plant was a daily turmoil of priority changes for goods in process and a need to have many kinds of garments in manufacture in small lots at the same time. Costs were raised excessively. Customers were alienated. Late deliveries led the sales people to accuse the manufacturing people of willful negligence and of misinformation; the plant people accused the others of carelessness in imposing impossible schedules. Quarrels and deep antagonisms had extended over a long time, and neither party seemed able to find a way to coordinate sales and production.

The effect of these conditions on the plant supervisor... was serious. They ignored the increased costs of... material due to small runs, rush deliveries... inventories. Production quotas were... regard to the frequent disruptions of... duce in required quantity, particular... peak, Weldon often had to hire inexper... short periods and to pay a guaranteed wa... which, for some lines and seasons, doubl... unit production cost. Supervisors felt justifi... set quota of dozens by every means within... kept both uninformed and unconcerned in... formance.

Work flow fluctuated widely, and workers som... from overtime to layoff in the same work wee... workers came to regard the plant as a place of s... occasional employment. Many would leave as soon... could find other jobs, while others would be discha... soon as the seasonal peak was past. Labor turnover th... high.

In the postwar transition from sellers' to buyers' market, ... consequences became drastic. Having retained outdated too...

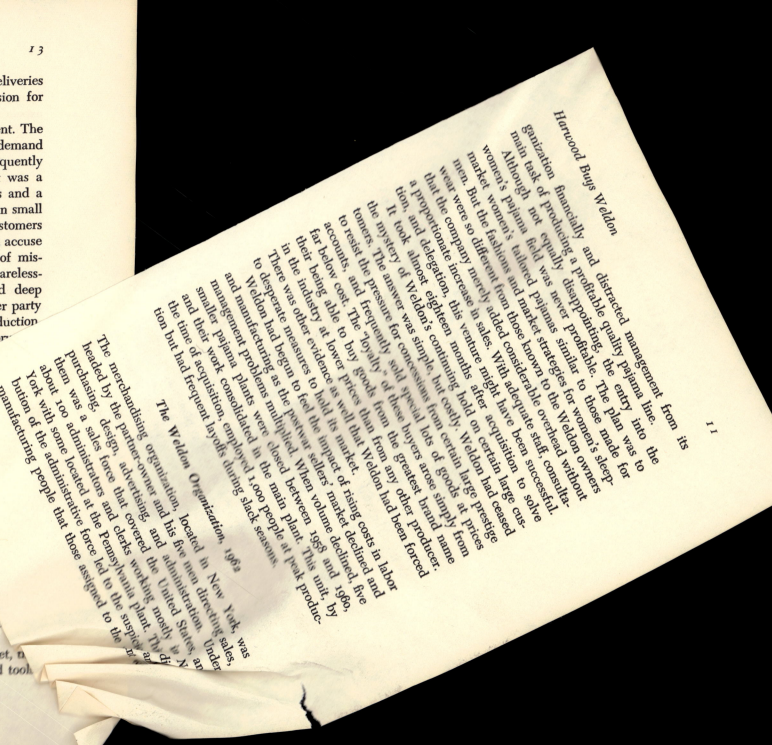

ganization financially and distracted management from its main task of producing a profitable quality pajama line. The plan was to make the entry into the women's sleepwear field, similar to those made for men. But the company merely added considerable overhead without a proportionate increase in sales. With adequate staff, consultation, and delegation, this venture might have been successful. The fashions and market strategies were so different from those known to the Weldon owners that the company never was able to hold on certain large prestige accounts after acquisition had ceased.

It took almost eighteen months after acquisition to solve the mystery of Weldon's continuing hold on certain large accounts, and frequently sold special lots of goods at prices far below cost. The "loyalty" of these buyers arose simply from their being able to buy goods from Weldon at prices far below cost, and frequently that Weldon had been forced to resist the pressure for concessions from certain large customers. The answer was simple, but costly. Weldon had begun to feel the impact of rising costs in labor and manufacturing problems multiplied. When volume declined, five smaller pajama plants were closed between 1958 and 1960, and their work consolidated in the main plant. This unit, by the time of acquisition, employed 1,000 people at peak production but had frequent layoffs during slack seasons.

The Weldon Organization, 1962

The merchandising organization, located in New York, was headed by the partner-owner and his five men directing sales, design, advertising, and administration. Under purchasing, there was a sales force that covered the United States, and them about 100 administrators and clerks working mostly in New York with some located at the Pennsylvania plant. The distribution of the administrative force led to the suspicion among manufacturing people that those assigned to the...

"spies" for the New York partner. In point of fact, they were employed in the plant primarily because salaries and related payroll costs were lower there than in New York.

The manufacturing division under the other partner-owner had five functional department heads. The plant organization, as in merchandising, was unbalanced, with too few people in management and supervision and too many in control and record-keeping. The imbalance was a result of the manager's effort to control activity through multiple and duplicating records. A large number of clerks were needed, also, because of inventory imbalances, to change shipping dates, suggest substitutions, and answer customer complaints.

Noteworthy gaps in staff and method were evident in the manufacturing division. A single industrial engineer with one assistant attempted to handle all problems of rate study and machine layout. Electronic data processing, although economically available, had not been introduced. There was no personnel department to provide essential records and services.

Within the total enterprise, the merchandising and manufacturing divisions functioned independently rather than as coordinated divisions of a single organization. Coordination was blocked by the clashes of temperament of the two partners and by the absence of any authorized coordination by others.

Moreover, each partner employed relatives in key positions. The son of the merchandising partner was employed as sales manager and a son-in-law as comptroller. A nephew of the manufacturing partner was employed as plant manager. Each "side" viewed the other with suspicion.

As a consequence, little communication ... between manufacture and sales. Manufacturing ... to see the other's problems, ... account of customer pressures upon ... designing divisions cre... complications ... models. S... that ...

and methods, Weldon forfeited its competitive advantage. Top management tried to counteract mounting losses by cutting expenditures for capital improvement so sharply that by 1962 even spare parts had to be taken from one machine to fix another. Weldon bought little new equipment and made little attempt to keep up with innovations in the tools or methods of manufacture. Their economies thus took a form that exaggerated rather than solved their production cost problems in the long run.

The partners seem to have believed that if they could hold their markets long enough they could find a way to cut costs to a profitable level. They took conventional steps to reduce payroll costs: cutting down on staff, withholding wage increases, calling on their people to make sacrifices, applying strong pressures. Costs did go down, for a time, and sales and production volume was maintained. But morale suffered, and these "economies" also began to add to cost.

With lowered morale came worry, anger, confusion, and fading of goodwill and cooperation. Costly delays mounted as the staff waited for top management to decide the most minuscule matters. Nor were the staff taken into the owners' confidence regarding plans for the future. The decision to sell Weldon came as a complete surprise to all but a few in the organization.

The Task of Rebuilding Weldon

Upon acquiring Weldon, and after the conditions I have described became known, Harwood faced the task of reshaping the organization without risking complete disruption. And, of course, the reshaping had to be undertaken concurrently with major technological changes. It had to be done quickly, to avoid loss of customers and continuing financial drain. It was not expected that success would come easily. Sacrifices, pains, and troubles were anticipated, but these had to be accepted if further setbacks and failure that would imperil the entire Weldon organization were to be avoided.

In my view at the time, the hardest challenge would be changing the practices of Weldon's managerial staff. They had to be developed into a team working together to achieve company goals. This meant for them a new way of accepting responsibility and exercising authority in a changed managerial framework.

Since labor costs count for 50 per cent of the selling price in this industry, human performance determines the success or failure of the company. Fortunately, we could fall back on studies, made in Harwood's plants, which had found some answers to problems of achieving lower costs, higher productivity, better performance, increased earnings, lowered turnover. The task, as I saw it, was to reshape Weldon's organizational policies and managerial approaches so that they followed the Harwood model.

Work methods were to be observed and improvements introduced where needed. Limited-purpose high-volume assembly lines were to replace the inefficient plantwide production flow. New equipment was to replace some of the outdated machinery, and modern work aids were to be added to eliminate some costly hand operations. Separate smaller departments, each operating on its own, were to perform all the operations to manufacture a finished product.

In addition, I thought it necessary to attempt some product standardization. Fewer models, with less frequent model changes, could ease the burden upon the supervisors and operators who had been dealing with an unnecessarily varied line of "custom made" models and styles.

Since Harwood staff could not be spared for these time-consuming tasks, a number of consultants were to be brought in. During the period 1962 to 1965 as many as five different consultants were in the plant at the same time. On their part, the consultants would have to recognize that they were to guide, not command, and that cooperation would come only as confidence was earned. As they kept discussing plans and programs with the Weldon staff, the early skepticism would change to trust, confidence, and improved performance.

This in brief was my view of the Weldon situation in mid-1962, some months after acquisition. What appeared at first to be a routine acquisition came to be seen more realistically as a task of rebuilding an enterprise that, for all its strengths, was then in difficulty and unable to help itself.

ganization financially and distracted management from its main task of producing a profitable quality pajama line.

Although not equally disappointing, the entry into the women's pajama field was never profitable. The plan was to market women's tailored pajamas similar to those made for men. But the fashions and market strategies for women's sleepwear were so different from those known to the Weldon owners that the company merely added considerable overhead without a proportionate increase in sales. With adequate staff, consultation, and delegation, this venture might have been successful.

It took almost eighteen months after acquisition to solve the mystery of Weldon's continuing hold on certain large customers. The answer was simple, but costly. Weldon had ceased to resist the pressure for concessions from certain large prestige accounts, and frequently sold special lots of goods at prices far below cost. The "loyalty" of these buyers arose simply from their being able to buy goods from the greatest brand name in the industry at lower prices than from any other producer. There was other evidence as well that Weldon had been forced to desperate measures to hold its market.

Weldon had begun to feel the impact of rising costs in labor and manufacturing as the postwar sellers' market declined and management problems multiplied. When volume declined, five smaller pajama plants were closed between 1958 and 1960, and their work consolidated in the main plant. This unit, by the time of acquisition, employed 1,000 people at peak production but had frequent layoffs during slack seasons.

The Weldon Organization, 1962

The merchandising organization, located in New York, was headed by the partner-owner and his five men directing sales, purchasing, design, advertising, and administration. Under them was a sales force that covered the United States, and about 100 administrators and clerks working mostly in New York with some located at the Pennsylvania plant. This distribution of the administrative force led to the suspicion among manufacturing people that those assigned to the plant were "spies" for the New York partner. In point of fact, they were employed in the plant primarily because salaries and related payroll costs were lower there than in New York.

The manufacturing division under the other partner-owner had five functional department heads. The plant organization, as in merchandising, was unbalanced, with too few people in management and supervision and too many in control and record-keeping. The imbalance was a result of the manager's effort to control activity through multiple and duplicating records. A large number of clerks were needed, also, because of inventory imbalances, to change shipping dates, suggest substitutions, and answer customer complaints.

Noteworthy gaps in staff and method were evident in the manufacturing division. A single industrial engineer with one assistant attempted to handle all problems of rate study and machine layout. There was no program of research and development. Electronic data processing, although economically available, had not been introduced. There was no personnel department to provide essential records and services.

Within the total enterprise, the merchandising and manufacturing divisions functioned independently rather than as coordinated divisions of a single organization. Coordination was blocked by the clashes of temperament of the two partners and by the absence of any authorized coordination by others. Moreover, each partner employed relatives in key positions. The son of the merchandising partner was employed as sales manager and a son-in-law as comptroller. A nephew of the manufacturing partner was employed as plant manager. Each "side" viewed the other with suspicion.

As a consequence, little communication was maintained between manufacture and sales. Each division became unable to see the other's problems. Manufacturing took little or no account of customer pressures upon the sales department. Sales and designing divisions made little effort to understand the plant complications created by an unrestricted variation of styles and models. Salesmen agreed too readily to sell any type of styling that customers requested without regard to what the plant could produce at a profit. Salesmen, who were generally paid on a commission basis, promised impossibly fast deliveries at mutually conflicting dates. There was little provision for coordination or plant clearance.

Production schedules were set by the sales department. The recurrent conflicts in delivery promises forced them to demand almost daily changes in production priorities and frequently to demand partial deliveries. The effect in the plant was a daily turmoil of priority changes for goods in process and a need to have many kinds of garments in manufacture in small lots at the same time. Costs were raised excessively. Customers were alienated. Late deliveries led the sales people to accuse the manufacturing people of willful negligence and of mis-information; the plant people accused the others of careless-ness in imposing impossible schedules. Quarrels and deep antagonisms had extended over a long time, and neither party seemed able to find a way to coordinate sales and production.

The effect of these conditions on the plant supervisory staff was serious. They ignored the increased costs of labor and material due to small runs, rush deliveries, and unbalanced inventories. Production quotas were set arbitrarily, without regard to the frequent disruptions of the work flow. To pro-duce in required quantity, particularly during the seasonal peak, Weldon often had to hire inexperienced employees for short periods and to pay a guaranteed wage for a low output which, for some lines and seasons, doubled and tripled the unit production cost. Supervisors felt justified in meeting the set quota of dozens by every means within reach, and were kept both uninformed and unconcerned in their cost per-formance.

Work flow fluctuated widely, and workers sometimes went from overtime to layoff in the same work week. Weldon workers came to regard the plant as a place of seasonal or occasional employment. Many would leave as soon as they could find other jobs, while others would be discharged as soon as the seasonal peak was past. Labor turnover thus was high.

In the postwar transition from sellers' to buyers' market, the consequences became drastic. Having retained outdated tools and methods, Weldon forfeited its competitive advantage. Top management tried to counteract mounting losses by cutting expenditures for capital improvement so sharply that by 1962 even spare parts had to be taken from one machine to fix another. Weldon bought little new equipment and made little attempt to keep up with innovations in the tools or methods of manufacture. Their economies thus took a form that exaggerated rather than solved their production cost problems in the long run.

The partners seem to have believed that if they could hold their markets long enough they could find a way to cut costs to a profitable level. They took conventional steps to reduce payroll costs: cutting down on staff, withholding wage increases, calling on their people to make sacrifices, applying strong pressures. Costs did go down, for a time, and sales and production volume was maintained. But morale suffered, and these "economies" also began to add to cost.

With lowered morale came worry, anger, confusion, and fading of goodwill and cooperation. Costly delays mounted as the staff waited for top management to decide the most minuscule matters. Nor were the staff taken into the owners' confidence regarding plans for the future. The decision to sell Weldon came as a complete surprise to all but a few in the organization.

The Task of Rebuilding Weldon

Upon acquiring Weldon, and after the conditions I have described became known, Harwood faced the task of reshaping the organization without risking complete disruption. And, of course, the reshaping had to be undertaken concurrently with major technological changes. It had to be done quickly, to avoid loss of customers and continuing financial drain. It was not expected that success would come easily. Sacrifices, pains, and troubles were anticipated, but these had to be accepted if further setbacks and failure that would imperil the entire Weldon organization were to be avoided.

2

THE WELDON PLANT
AND ORGANIZATION

*John R. Nelson**

I FIRST SAW the Weldon manufacturing facilities in August
1961 as an exchange visitor. Such exchanges are common in
the industry. At the time, negotiations for purchase had begun.
My assignment, known only to the top managers of Weldon
and Harwood, was to look over the plant, its operations, the
work force, the supervisory and management group, their
methods, and their equipment. My report was favorable, on
the whole. By the following January the sale was completed.
I then made several visits to the Weldon plant, at first to review
the situation further as a representative of the new ownership,
and later to take a more active part in planning and initiating
needed changes.

From the outset I felt that opportunities existed for sizable
savings in manufacturing. While I was struck immediately by
certain deficiencies, it seemed clear that the basic facilities
were sound, or could be made so, and that there were at
Weldon people who knew how to make a good product.

The plant building itself was impressive in size and suitability, although old and not well maintained. The available
floor space in relation to production volume was greater than

---

* Vice president for manufacturing, the Harwood Manufacturing
Corporation.

at any of the Harwood plants, and the possibilities were good for flexible rearrangement and for movement of goods.

There was a striking lack of modern equipment and machinery, and Weldon obviously had not kept up with some of the methods and work aids that had proven their cost-saving value in Harwood plants and elsewhere. For example, some of their finishing operations were done with methods that involved a great deal of hand work at a cost twice as great as that elsewhere. I estimated that improved equipment and work methods throughout the plant could reduce costs as much as 15 per cent while at the same time allowing potential increases in employee earnings of 20 to 30 per cent.

The plant layout and work flow were far from optimum. A single large finishing department handled the output from all the sewing rooms. Each of the sewing rooms handled a wide variety of styles and materials. Movement of work in process was excessive, and the amount of semifinished work on hand was so great as to crowd even a rather spacious plant. Operators did much of their own bundle searching and moving, and this added to the confusion. Conversion to a "unit" system, with smaller and complete departments each with its own space and its own limited range of styles, would help to improve the work flow and would bring other gains as well.

In all parts of the plant there was unnecessary paperwork connected with the processing and control of orders. It appeared that improved order control and simplification of records would give significant savings.

Weldon had a history of difficulty in maintaining balanced production lines. This arose from many causes. For example, the mixing of different styles in the same assembly line made it difficult to keep each operator continuously on work for which she was best qualified. There were frequent rush jobs and priority changes that prevented holding to a schedule and caused considerable shifting of operators from their regular jobs to new ones. Worst of all, high absence and turnover rates meant that there were many inexperienced operators, who could not hold to the scheduled output pace; and each morning there were a number of vacancies to be filled by temporary transfer of people from their regular jobs. The daily absence rate at the time of one of my early visits was 7 per cent, and the monthly turnover of employees was 12 per cent—both figures extremely high for the industry. Along with the technical difficulties that come with frequent job changes, the operators and supervisors had little chance to develop familiar friendship patterns and work rhythms; this in turn aggravated the absence and turnover problem.

In spite of these difficulties, the Weldon plant was turning out a reasonably good product and succeeded in filling its orders, although often late and at high cost.

Turning from the plant and technology to the staff, there were again observations both favorable and unfavorable. I was impressed by the willingness of the operators to show an outsider what they were doing and how they were going about it. There was little friction evident between the operators. Each operator set her own pace, and the work arrangements did not cause the slow workers to handicap the faster ones. The work force included a core of highly skilled employees along with a larger group of "floaters" and low-skilled employees.

For their part, the supervisors and managers were skilled technically and appeared to be dedicated to their work. They knew a great deal about the manufacturing process, what equipment to use, what made the equipment run well, what made a good or bad product. The top manufacturing people also had these technical skills—they were personally familiar with the details of making garments. This seemed at times to distract them from managerial problems. For example, during my first visit, while in conversation in a sewing room with the plant manager and his production manager, a number of operators came up to ask the production manager for approval or help on minor matters. Later observations confirmed that the employees often felt unable to do things without specific approval and that a great deal of top managerial time went into direct floor supervision.

However, the "supervisors" were not acting as supervisors in the normal sense, as professional managers understand the term. They were primarily floor help or group leaders, responsible for seeing that goods moved through the department during the day. They made few real decisions and assumed little responsibility for anything other than the immediate floor problems that came up. The supervision, such as it was, came from the production manager himself, who spent most of his day running (actually running) through the sewing rooms giving morning orders to each supervisor and repeating the rounds to see that his directions were being carried out. He personally passed on most issues of quality or priority or work assignment, and the like, that came up during the day.

I felt at the time, and this was confirmed later, that these so-called supervisors could really supervise if given the opportunity. They were familiar with the plant's problems, its equipment, the styles, and the people. Their performance was better than might have been expected in view of the fact that they were not given the information or the time needed to understand the full range of supervisory responsibilities. I felt confident that we would be able to keep all of them. We would have to add to their number, as there were not enough supervisors for the volume of work. Also, they would have to learn a great deal about things they had not been allowed to concern themselves about—such vital matters as lost time, delay time, unit earnings, forward planning, employee training, and many others.

At all levels in the organization there was a weakness arising from the combination of authoritarian methods and traditions with insufficient staff. The plant management and supervisory group as a whole was rather large in number, but only a few of them were actually engaged in controlling the work system and in forward planning for cost improvement, and these few were terribly overworked. They were bogged down in detail even while they had lower-level people who were potentially competent, but devoid of authority to do obviously needed things.

Against this background, the Weldon change program at the plant was undertaken. In my view the order of visible changes —first technological and later social—was determined by the

obvious need to cut costs in the short run. This called for in-
stalling improved work aids and machines and some major
work flow improvements as rapidly as possible. This priority
also arose because I felt that Weldon had some staff resources
for dealing with technical matters, and practically no resources
for dealing with human organization. In addition, I felt that
the tangible changes in the work would provide a background
and means for the social changes.

The deficit in managerial and supervisory staff would have
to be met from outside for a time. Various consultants would
be needed not only for expert advice but also for direct help
to and training of the Weldon people at all levels. The consultants would have to work not only with top management
but also with people right down to the production workers. As
it turned out later, we had a number of consultants of different
kinds, often at the same time. It is remarkable that their activities fitted together, for any one manager or supervisor might
during a given period be working with three or four different
"outside" people on such matters as equipment, layout, work
method, piece rates, training, production reports, and others.
I think this intense infusion of outside help succeeded because
we emphasized always the involvement of Weldon people in
the changes that developed and emphasized the authority of
the regular Weldon people in their different areas.

From the beginning at Weldon, if a change involved operators, they were to be consulted directly. We were particularly
interested in talking with many Weldon people about current
plans and activities, and this interaction among employees,
visiting Harwood staff, and the technical consultants helped
to build a foundation for the consultants on social change who
came in later.

Had the social changes been emphasized first, I doubt that
the program at Weldon would have been as successful. Most
people, particularly in a plant of this type, appreciate technical
competence. Another order of change would probably have
appeared too theoretical or academic, whereas changes in the
physical work situation were tangible and within their con-

cerns at that time. In addition, the technical changes provided actual problems to discuss, so that meetings and counseling sessions could be "for real" and not just an exercise.

At the same time, we wanted an emphasis during the early technical activities upon consultation, local responsibility, planning, and coordination among staff. This provided the Weldon people—often for the first time in their lives—with some personal experience with the principles we had to build into the social organization. In this sense the technical and social changes at Weldon were to be interwoven right from the start.

THE HARWOOD
ORGANIZATION

Alfred J. Marrow

IN CONFRONTING the situation presented by the acquisition of Weldon and the need for a program of change, the Harwood company could draw on its own experiences. Since 1939, Harwood had been involved in applying the postulates of group dynamics to the problems of management. This nearly continuous work in research and application—from 1939 until the present—provides a scientifically grounded and practical-ity-tested basis for the improvement of an organization. This background, and the ideas developed from it, were made available to Weldon.

In mid-1962 we started an active program to rebuild the Weldon organization. The Harwood organization became the model for this change program—partly because it was success-ful under conditions similar to those faced by Weldon and partly, no doubt, because Harwood embodied the values and assumptions as well as the practical experience of the new Weldon owners.

The Harwood plants became centers of behavioral research when the late Professor Kurt Lewin began working with the plant management in 1939 on problems of leadership training, group decision, interpersonal relations, and group dynamics.[1] In the years thereafter, he continued working with the Harwood owners and later brought in such coworkers as Alex Bavelas and John R. P. French, Jr., to carry out a number of pioneering action-research projects.

The stage was initially set for Harwood's long-term involvement in action research when in 1939 the company opened a new plant in a small Virginia community. Harwood was a family concern that had been founded in 1899 by a self-made entrepreneur who went into business with a capital of $1,000, partly saved, partly borrowed. A personable man and benevolent manager, he had limited technical knowledge and survived on a marginal basis in a highly competitive line of business. In the late 1930s, management of the company was turned over to his two sons—one a psychologist, the other an engineer—and it was they who directed the move south. It then became company policy to apply scientific knowledge to the problems of management in order to bring about more satisfying employee relationships and a more willing and active cooperation in day-to-day work.

About three years after opening its new Virginia plant, Harwood experienced problems in developing an expanded work force. World War II had created a manpower shortage, and Harwood was confronted with changing the traditional aversion of its supervisors toward employing "older" workers. Growing labor shortages made it necessary to employ older people; yet such hiring was resisted. At the time this was a critical issue to the company, and it is a problem that illustrates how Harwood has learned some things about management.

Dr. John R. P. French, Jr., was then director of personnel research for the company. He cited scientific proof that older people did have the kinds of skills and aptitudes required for the jobs in this plant, but the staff attitude remained unchanged. Dr. French realized that merely telling the staff that their attitude was contrary to the facts would not persuade

---

[1] A. J. Marrow, *Making Management Human*, New York, McGraw-Hill, 1957.

them. It would have been easy to impose a new hiring policy, but it was felt that this approach would be self-defeating. He concluded that it was necessary for the staff to unlearn their mistaken beliefs and that this would occur only if they would seek out the facts for themselves. Only then could they recognize the discrepancy between facts and belief.

Accordingly, Dr. French sought to involve the staff members in research of their own. A modest project was suggested to them. If older workers were inefficient, it would be advisable to determine how much money the company was losing by continuing the employment of those older women who were already in the plant. There were a number of such women, those who had several years of service, or who had been taken on more recently as a favor to the community—a widow, possibly, or a hardship case.

Full responsibility for designing the project was placed, not with the research director, but with the members of the management staff. They were to determine the best methods of collecting data. The project was theirs, not his, and so would be the credit. They could come up with something which was of their own devising.

The findings were in sharp contrast to the staff's expectations. Not age, but other factors, determined success or failure on the job. But the analysis being their own, the staff trusted it. Thus being enabled to re-examine their beliefs through first-hand exploration, they were helped to new understanding. In the process, they "unlearned" some of the beliefs they had been convinced were true and were now ready to affirm quite different ones. They also learned something about the value of research applied to organizational problems.[2]

This experiment is a good example of the kind of action research that Lewin advocated and that Harwood used when feasible. It points up that when members of a group take part in a fact-finding inquiry of this sort, the very circumstance that the findings are their own inspires them to change their

---

[2] A. J. Marrow and J. R. P. French, Jr., "Changing a Stereotype in Industry," *Journal of Social Issues*, December 1945, pp. 33–37.

attitude and subsequent behavior. As Lewin put it, "This result occurs because the facts become really their facts (as against other people's facts). An individual will believe facts he himself has discovered in the same way that he believes in himself." When the findings are their own, people cannot challenge them as inadequate, or impute any bias to the fact-finders. They then recognize they must have been mistaken before.

Participative Management

Since its early involvement with participative management practices in cooperation with behavioral scientists Harwood's management has been convinced that a job is done best when employees feel that their needs are considered in a way that sustains their self-respect and creates a sense of responsibility. As employees they "participate." They do not feel the humiliation implied in the term "hired hands." They do not feel they are mere robots. But their "participation," Harwood learned, must be consistent with what is feasible and must be realistic in terms of the work to be done. They are not asked to "decide" on anything unless the decision is really up to them. If it is not, they may be asked for their counsel, but not their consent. The distinction is clearly made, in discussing problems with them, between "we'd like your opinion" and "the final decision is going to be up to you."

The question is often asked: Have the workers' opinions been of much value? That depends on how much the participator knows and how important the matter is to him. On matters which the workers know best—their own jobs, conditions in the shop, operation of machines—they have far more informed opinions than top managers who lack first-hand experience. Harwood found that workers can make practical suggestions of considerable merit. Many are ingenious and inventive, capable of seeing short cuts, and aware of their own and their fellow workers' capabilities.

As an illustration, consider an operator who sews pockets on men's shirts. Under current manufacturing processes, an experienced worker will sew well over 100,000 pockets every year. The group of which she is a member may jointly sew a million pockets a year. Is it not reasonable to expect, at least within the limits of their own direct experience and observations, that they are more expert in the details of their particular job than any of the supervisory staff?

Harwood's management has learned from its experiences that the method of participation need not always be formalized. A meeting does not always have to be called, with everyone sitting around a conference table. A foreman walking through his department can develop ideas and solutions informally with his subordinates or production workers while they are on the job. In fact, such constant informal contact and consultation makes participation an integral part of the day's work.

But a participative approach to problem-solving can succeed only when there is mutual confidence. Then employees and managers are trusting and open, and problems can be approached in a spirit of joint inquiry and a consensus worked out. Harwood found that participation leads to more loyalty, more flexibility, and more efficiency. Relationships on the job shift from competition to cooperation. A sense of mutual interdependence develops.

To test these concepts at the rank-and-file level, Dr. French set up an experiment that both corroborated and illustrated the Harwood management approach. The experiment was done at a Harwood plant which was making a number of changes in machines and operations methods.[3] The changes were strongly resisted by workers, many of whom were being transferred to new jobs in other departments. They expressed their resentment in several ways: by complaints about new piecework rates, by quitting, by restricting output, and by marked aggression toward the management.

Despite the adverse effect on morale, Harwood's management had no choice; with each season's change in styles and

---

[3] L. Coch and J. R. P. French, Jr., "Overcoming Resistance to Change," *Human Relations*, Vol. I, No. 4, 1948, pp. 512–532.

product mix, methods and jobs had to be altered, making it necessary to transfer employees to new jobs. While an incentive-pay plan was in force and the new job procedures usually resembled the old, the slightest changes proved often to be upsetting to workers on highly repetitive jobs. In re-action, skilled workers needlessly lengthened the learning time. Veteran workers when transferred took about twice as long as new workers to reach a standard rate—an obvious sign of resistance. When there were large-scale transfers, as many as 6o per cent of the workers quit. The turnover rate in such departments was three times greater than in departments which did not have to make job shifts. When transferred, the employees reacted to changes with "fight or flight." It is my impression that this is generally true throughout industry.

Special subsidy bonuses to workers over the relearning period did not help. Supervisors failed when they tried to cajole them into stepping up production to former levels. Union appeals for cooperation were also in vain. Meanwhile, the costly and irritating turnover persisted.

On analysis, it seemed that the operators felt they had lost face when upon job transfer their rating as skilled employees went down. They resented leaving their old group to join workers on other jobs in unfamiliar situations. Many com-plained. When ratings of daily performances were posted, those once at the top of the list and proud to be there were no longer there. A high percentage of those shifted more than once never regained their high places on the performance list. They gave up trying.

Against this background, the "participation" experiment was instituted. The workers were divided into three groups, all of them matched in skill, and were advised of the impending job changes in different ways.

Group I was called into the conference room and told that changes were to be made and why they were necessary. The production manager explained the new mode of work, the new job assignments, and the new piecework rates. The opera-tors were invited to ask questions and were given frank an-swers. By and large, this was normal procedure.

Group II workers were asked to choose representatives to meet with management to discuss and decide upon the new job methods. They were given a full explanation of why the change was mandatory—orders had fallen off for the style currently in production. Unless fresh business was attracted by new models and lower prices, there might be layoffs. The urgency of cutting costs by simplifying the product was dramatized as vividly as possible. The group was asked to discuss cost reduction as a joint problem of management and workers. The situation was defined this way: "We don't want to sacrifice quality, and we don't want you to lose any income. What ideas do you have about this?" The group's spokesmen brought the workers' views to management, joined in outlining new methods, and then went back to their fellow workers to explain the new job methods and rates and to help in the retraining.

Group III did not delegate decision-making to representatives but participated as a whole. Management and all the operators sat together from the start until the methods and rates were agreed upon. Though no formal vote was taken, the decisions were reached by consensus at the meetings.

What resulted from this three-pronged experiment? Production by Group I—the nonparticipative group—dropped 35 per cent after the changeover and did not improve for a month thereafter. Morale deteriorated; and there was marked hostility toward the company, restriction of output, subtle noncooperation. It turned out later that an agreement to "get even" with management had been explicitly made. Within two weeks after the change, 9 per cent of the operators had quit. Others filed grievances about the pay rates, although the rates were in fact a little too high.

Group II learned the new methods at a remarkably fast pace. Morale was good, and the standard rate of productivity was recovered within fourteen days. By the end of the month, productivity had exceeded what it had been before the changeover. The same supervisor whom Group I was criticizing received friendly cooperation from Group II. No one from Group II quit.

Group III, the fully participating group, took the lead from the start. By the second day, the operators were back to their former level of production and steadily raised it to a point about 14 per cent higher than ever before. They cooperated with their supervisor, and no one quit. Their excellent morale reflected their feeling that they were a team.

Two and a half months later, it was possible to confirm the results dramatically. Group I, which had to be broken up after six weeks because its low rate of production persisted, was reassembled when another new job opened up in the plant. But this time the change was made with full participation of all the members. The results were successful and the opposite of the earlier experience. There was rapid recovery after change-over: a new and higher level of output, no hostility, no terminations, high cooperation and morale.

In illustrating the managerial approach that has evolved in the company's development, Harwood's experiments also epitomize the human side of the management picture everywhere. Wages and hours are only part of that picture; the work climate must satisfy a range of human needs. Clearly, the findings are relevant to industry at a time when manufacturing methods and technology are changing with dramatic speed. These changes influence the attitude and behavior of the workers as they respond to frequent and often upsetting changes.

The Harwood experiences, of which only two are cited above, are characteristic of a growing body of findings. They demonstrate that the success of a modern enterprise depends upon motivating the people in the enterprise to accept responsibility, to work together, and thus to maximize their performance and their own well-being.

Despite an increased awareness of these facts of organization life, a management system that is often self-defeating still predominates. It is the traditional authoritarian system. The term "authoritarian" is currently unpopular because of its political implications, and many chief executives strongly object to such a description of the managerial system of their organizations even though their practices, as seen by their employees, are unmistakably authoritarian.

Doubts persist among managers in regard to the increasing number of planned change programs aimed toward *less* bureaucratic and *more* participative "open system" and adaptive structures. These doubts may arise from misconceptions based on past experience. They may stem from an assumption that arbitrary boundaries exist between management systems, so that any two systems are mutually exclusive. The fact is, there are gradations of practice, and it is primarily a matter of convenience in discussion to divide managerial approaches into the two opposites: the "authoritarian," based on centralized control and direction with strong individual leadership, and the "participative," based on shared responsibility and group collaboration.

In recent years many people in management have become familiar with three different but related ways for describing managerial approaches. These are (1) Rensis Likert's "Systems 1, 2, 3 and 4," with 1 being based on extreme authoritarian principles and 4 on the greatest degree of participation; (2) Robert Blake's "Managerial Grid Scale," 9:9 to 9:1, with 9:9 corresponding to equally strong concern for production and people and 9:1 a concern for production only; and (3) Douglas McGregor's "Theory X" for the authoritarian approach and "Theory Y" for the participative approach.[4] McGregor's formulation is psychological in origin and has received considerable favorable attention from other psychologists.

Most companies still operate on some variation of Theory X, as did the Weldon organization. But their approach is based on assumptions about human behavior and human nature that the psychologists tell us are contrary to their knowledge and research. Many companies operating on these principles were

---

[4] R. Likert, *New Patterns of Management*, New York, McGraw-Hill, 1961. R. R. Blake and Jane S. Mouton, *The Managerial Grid*, Houston, Texas, Gulf Publishing Co., 1964. D. McGregor, *The Human Side of Enterprise*, New York, McGraw-Hill, 1960.

successful in the past and are successful now, but to continue growing they must reshape their policies and introduce less authoritarian management practices. This is being made increasingly necessary by the vast changes taking place in modern society—changes in education, changes in living standards, and changes in technology.

In American society, the young adult accepts the fact that he must work to live, and looks forward eagerly to his first job. But as soon as he starts to work, he finds in most cases that life in the work environment is so overorganized and so overcontrolled that he is kept in a state of supervised conformity. Though his home and education may have prepared him for self-discipline and shared responsibility, job rules and regulations treat him as though he were irresponsible and undisciplined.

In the present era of full employment, managers are learning that employee cooperation and performance can be neither coerced nor bought—their loyalty must be won. No leader can step up production, lift morale, or create unity by simple fiat. The hero of Eugene O'Neill's *Marco Millions* is a true authoritarian. He cannot understand why there should be unrest in the empire where he rules as Kubla Khan's minister, since, as he says: "I've passed a law that everyone should be happy." Marco is a symbol of the paternalistic employer whose benevolence does not produce the results he intends.

The effect of a different approach, one striving for participation, is evident to visitors in the Harwood plants. Managers at all levels do indeed manage. They are trained to assume responsibility and are given the necessary authority. The general maturity and self-sufficiency of the members of supervision are noteworthy; except for unusual circumstances, day-to-day supervision by higher levels of management is at a minimum.

Basically, Harwood has approached its problems with the assumption that employees want the same things that their employers do. If employees are jealous of their prerogatives and status, so are executives. If they set up featherbedding practices, so do the men in the top office. If they want more money, so do the president and vice president of the company. On the other hand, employees are unlikely to rebel against decisions they themselves helped to make (a fact which is consistent with many findings in psychotherapy). People must have a hand in helping themselves; they cannot and will not be helped exclusively from the outside.

Harwood is now the largest company in its field. With the acquisition of Weldon, it produces about 20 per cent of the world supply of its specialized product. While many factors enter into the successful operation of an organization, it is the opinion of the Harwood owners that their managerial approach has played a major part in bringing their company to the foremost position in the industry.

Against this background of the principles guiding the Harwood management, the company was confronted with the problem of making extensive changes in the leadership styles, technology, and the managerial practices and controls in the Weldon firm. What began as an acquisition for financial investment became—for practical reasons—an unprecedented opportunity for a systematic study of planned organizational change. It was a business decision to undertake a participative approach to the salvaging of the Weldon enterprise; it was a more personal decision to use the situation to learn more about the value of participative management and about the process of purposely creating a desired kind of organizational life with the Weldon people.

4

WELDON VS. AMALGAMATED CLOTHING WORKERS

Hyman Kornbluh[*]

THE GREAT SURGE of organization of unskilled and semiskilled workers started in the early 1930s under the National Industrial Recovery Act. Though it was later to be declared unconstitutional, its provisions for the first time gave workers the right to organize into unions and obligated employers to bargain with them. Coupled with the depressed conditions and low wages of the Great Depression, the favorable governmental atmosphere ignited the explosion in union growth. The Wagner Act was passed in 1935, providing more comprehensive protection for the growth of unions; and dur-

---

[*] Associate Director, Institute of Labor and Industrial Relations, the University of Michigan–Wayne State University. Formerly business agent with the Pennsylvania Joint Board, Amalgamated Clothing Workers of America. The author is solely responsible for the contents of this chapter. However, he wishes to thank the following for their time and patience in reconstructing events, giving information and making records available, all of which made the writing of the chapter possible: David J. Monas, vice president, ACWA, and manager, Pennsylvania Joint Board, Shirt Workers Union; Peter Swoboda, vice president, ACWA, and assistant manager, Pennsylvania Joint Board, Shirt Workers Union; Delmont Mileski, field director, Union Label Department, ACWA; and Valentine Wertheimer, assistant general secretary-treasurer, ACWA.

ing the following five years, 5 million workers flocked to the newly formed CIO (Congress of Industrial Organizations) and to the many unions that remained in the AFL (American Federation of Labor), adapting their structure to admit the mass-production worker.

The period during World War II saw further significant unionization. As the government and the country pressured for uninterrupted production for the war effort, the union movement yielded its right to strike and gained a more favorable atmosphere for peacefully achieving recognition and adjusting bargaining differences.

During the late forties and the 1950s, there came a maturing of relationships on the industrial scene as unions and managements adjusted to the idea of living with each other. Longer-term contracts began to emerge as the pattern. Fringe benefits received increasing attention, and binding arbitration became institutionalized for settling contract interpretation disputes. Some of the focus of conflict moved into the legislative halls. Possibly excepting the immediate post-World War II period, the turbulence of the last half of the thirties did not recur.

A key union in the formation of the CIO was the Amalgamated Clothing Workers of America (ACWA), which had broken away from the United Garment Workers in 1914. Operating in a highly competitive and seasonal industry, the union under the leadership of Sidney Hillman developed the first major grievance and arbitration machinery, which was used as a model in industrial relations for many other industries. The ACWA has long had a philosophy of attempting to bring stability to a historically chaotic industry in order to gain decent wages and working conditions for employees by limiting the ravages of cutthroat competition. Its approach to labor relations included close cooperation in the modernizing of production in organized plants to keep them competitive, the extending of loans through the Amalgamated Bank to some union-contract employers to help them through temporary difficulties, and early attempts to help form and bargain with employers' associations to provide standardization of agreements. The ACWA pioneered in instituting unemployment insurance, health, welfare, and other fringe benefits in manufacturing industries.

The ink was hardly dry on the National Industrial Recovery Act when the ACWA put every available organizer into the field. Key targets were the enclaves of "runaway shops" in the areas surrounding the large East Coast cities. By moving to depressed farm and coal regions in the 1920s and early 1930s, these companies had tapped small-town and rural sources of cheap labor while escaping from the union strongholds in the big cities.

One such area was the anthracite region of Pennsylvania, which contained many cotton garment shops. Working in these shops were the wives and daughters of miners who had a background of prolonged and intense struggle for unionization in the hard-coal industry. In Wilkes-Barre, Hazletown, Pottsville, and other towns, the fire caught on as the ACWA organizers crystallized the pent-up feelings of workers laboring under severely depressed work and wage conditions (wages in some cases came to 10 cents an hour). At times, a union organizer found himself sought out by a committee of workers to lead them in a strike which had already started.

Out of the drive came the formation of the Pennsylvania Joint Board, Shirt Workers Union, of the ACWA, the regional structure of the union embracing the men's cotton garment plants in the eastern part of the state. Within this territory was the town which from 1932 on housed the main plant of the firm later to be named the Weldon Manufacturing Company. But the union's drive did not reach this plant, and the organizing of Weldon was not to take place for almost three more decades. In the interim, the Weldon workers, and the ACWA, experienced extreme hostility on the part of management toward unionization. The union attempted a number of organizing drives and called one abortive strike. Some years later, the union was to use an extensive consumer education campaign to bring pressure on the company to halt its anti-union efforts. With the loss of a subsequent representation election, the union finally achieved recognition in 1963 after the purchase of Weldon by Harwood. The result was a complete turnabout in the management-union-worker relationship in the plant, which is built today on a mutually cooperative approach within the framework of a modernized production system.

The Weldon plant was located in a large building that had housed a rubber goods factory during the 1920s. When the rubber plant left in 1930, a civic committee conducted a drive to attract new business into the city. Weldon was the first to move into the building, in 1932. It was eventually followed by ten other small firms, all of them manufacturing soft goods.

Through the thirties and early forties, the ACWA made sporadic attempts at organizing the plant. A full-scale campaign never developed, however, since the organizers who probed the situation found a depressed town with no background of unionism, and widespread fear that unionization would only result in loss of jobs. Whenever an organizer was known to be in town, Weldon's anti-union management shut off the machines, started rumors that the plant would move if the union came in, and made intimidating speeches. ACWA Joint Board officials have stated that the company's methods for playing on workers' fears were the worst they encountered in the Pennsylvania area.

By the mid-forties, it was apparent to the union that the Weldon Company presented very formidable obstacles to organizing efforts. First was the company's demonstrated determination and ability to withstand them. The firm was now one of the larger units in an industry otherwise characterized by small-scale plants, and it was one of the better-financed organizations. It had the resources and the will to do a more sophisticated and professional job of resisting unionization.

Second, the geography of the plant itself made it difficult to concentrate solely on Weldon workers. Eleven firms occupied the building, some of which were in the ACWA's jurisdiction. With employees of all the firms using twelve different gate entrances to a structure occupying a large square city block, it was difficult to distinguish the workers from any one company. Large financial and personnel resources were necessary to cover the building for distribution of leaflets and, as was shown later, for picketing during a strike. In addition, during most of the 1940s and 1950s, the firm had three other smaller plants in Pennsylvania and controlled a plant in Gulfport, Mississippi, which gave it flexibility in shifting work when necessary.

Thus the union concluded that the key to organizing Weldon was to attempt a coordinated campaign with other unions aimed at organizing all the shops in the building.

In 1947, two organizers were assigned to the general area. Having successfully organized a cotton garment shop in a nearby town, they moved into the Weldon situation. Although there were attempts to approach the firms sharing Weldon's building as a totality through the local CIO Council, a sustained drive did not materialize. According to the organizers' report, the following were the main fears of the Weldon workers and workers in the other firms in the building:

1. Fear that the plants would move out
2. Fear that the boss would find out that the employee had joined the union
3. Fear of a strike

A recent strike by another union in a nearby ladies' garment plant emphasized this last fear. Although the organizers did make some headway in two of the smaller shops in the building, one of them closed down for a period during the union drive and stirred fears of job loss throughout the building. In the other case, although a large majority of the employees had signed up to join the union, the ACWA could get nowhere in attempting to negotiate with the employer. Restricted from using the election processes of the National Labor Relations Board (the ACWA, along with some other unions, refused on principle for a time to comply with the non-Communist affidavit provisions of the newly passed Taft-Hartley Law), the union attempted to negotiate an agreement with the employer, but to no avail. Thus a possible foothold in the building was lost. In addition, some of the Weldon pieceworkers may have been earning higher wages than the employees in the low-wage shops in the building, a factor which perhaps affected their attitudes toward the union.

In December 1950 a full-fledged campaign aimed specifically at the Weldon operation began. A full-time organizer was assigned to the drive, assisted by business agents from the ACWA Pennsylvania Joint Board. Within two months, the drive had progressed to the point where apparently more than one-third of the 700 eligible employees were signed up.

In response to these initial successes, the company employed a tactic frequently used to thwart organizing drives. It announced a general wage increase. The union countered by charging that the increase was not given to all employees.

However, the union's campaign was short-circuited. On February 19, 1951, an episode took place of the type that can often trigger a walkout. A trimmer, whose wife was expecting a child, was fired. His fellow workers in the cutting room, one of the prounion strongholds in the plant, attributed this to his union activities. When they approached management, they were told to accept the firing or leave. About two-thirds of the employees in the cutting room walked out, joined by some women from the sewing rooms.

With much trepidation that this was too early in the campaign to rally the support needed for such a strike, the union nevertheless backed the strikers who voted to convert the walkout to a strike for union recognition. Picket lines were set up, manned by up to 150 pickets, although these were not enough to cover effectively all the entrances to the building. The union estimated that at the peak of the strike about half the Weldon employees stayed home.

By the fifth week, it was clear that the company was not being hurt enough to give in to demands for union recognition. The union then approached the management in order to obtain the best possible arrangement for ending the strike. The strikers had been fired and some new persons hired. Union records show a form indicating that those who had not reported to work were notified that their jobs were terminated. The union tried to find jobs for those who were not reinstated after the strike was ended. According to the union, those strikers who were rehired eventually left or were weeded out by the company.

In the Weldon campaign, as in other drives to organize a plant of this size, the union did not use full-time or even part-time resources on a continuing basis. Instead, it maintained contact with the more active people in the plant and kept informed on upcoming plant issues. Then, in 1956, the union decided to commit more resources to see whether a campaign could develop. The brief attempt made in 1956 never reached the point of an election.

In 1959, the ACWA resumed its organizing campaign at Weldon and filed an NLRB petition for an election. Meanwhile, as the NLRB broadened its policy on employer response to an organizing campaign, the company wrote a number of letters to the employees, opposing the union drive. For example, on September 2, 1959, the plant manager and vice president wrote a letter to the employees, playing skillfully on employee recollections of the 1951 strike. It stated in part:

> As I promised you in the past, I'll answer all rumors that are being spread by the union, for the purpose of keeping you informed of the truth. . . . We have heard it said that the union is going to call a *RECOGNITION STRIKE*. If they do, they will put up a picket line at the entrance, but, if that happens, you do not need to fear the pickets. We are going to keep our doors open and continue to operate this plant. We have every confidence that the vast majority of our employees will not be part of such strike activities. *A RECOGNITION STRIKER* can be replaced, and if they are effectively replaced, they will have no jobs when the strike ends. . . . We have had a very good *steady work record*, and I firmly believe that, if the union comes into the picture, it will seriously effect this *good work record*, because unions when they disagree with management, call strikes. . . .

This letter reflected the dynamic impact of a lost strike. The strike into which the union was forced eight years earlier presented a major deterrent to unionizing efforts in 1959.

Although it had a substantial number of workers signed up, the union withdrew its petition for an election and undertook instead, in January 1960, a consumer education program. Letters were written to leading department store outlets, and a publicity campaign was aimed at other union members and the public. Later, pickets were assigned to department stores in major cities. The campaign used such slogans as "If you're sleeping in a Weldon, you're sleeping under a cloud," and "Lullaby without the label." This effort created bad will toward the Weldon company among many retailers, who complained of the unfavorable publicity resulting from pickets marching all day in front of their main entrances.

While the consumer education campaign was going on, another ACWA organizing campaign began in 1960 at the plant, and an NLRB election was set for May 18, 1961. In the meantime (January 1961), the firm had closed one of its nearby plants, blaming this on the union's consumer campaign. The union was chagrined since union sentiment was stronger in the closed plant than in the main plant in Williamsport. The union was also in a ticklish situation: Under the circumstances, workers could perceive the consumer education campaign either as hurting or helping them. In addition, although the Joint Board officials felt the consumer campaign was affecting the company's sales, they also felt that the company was now suffering from increasing mismanagement.

However, the union cause got a lift when a major shirt producer opened a plant in Williamsport and signed a contract under their arrangement with the ACWA in their other plants. Since this new firm was known for running a well-managed plant with a labor relations policy of mutual respect, the union felt it now had a strong base in Williamsport from which to build an eventual victory at Weldon. Nonetheless, in the 1961 election, the vote was in the company's favor, with the union getting 37 per cent of the ballots.

Within months following the election, the Harwood company acquired the Weldon company, signaling a new approach for the union. Aware of Harwood's more enlightened management and labor policies, the ACWA dampened its attack on the company and launched an intensive house-to-house campaign to sign up employees. One union leaflet, for instance, argued that the plant now had a management that had recognized unions in its other plants and urged employees to get organized representation and the accompanying benefits. The union plant committee and the organizers stopped attacking the Weldon Company and began instead a hard effort to persuade the employees that it would now be safe for them to sign up with the union if they so desired.

Meanwhile, Weldon under new ownership was reorganizing the production processes in the plant. While the effect of vast plant changes on worker morale probably added to prounion sentiment during the early period of reorganization, officials of the ACWA were aware that a more efficient and better-managed plant could eventually benefit the work force.

After a year and a half of organizing efforts with a four-man staff, the union had strong worker support and a solid organizational base. In November 1963, the union petitioned the company for official acceptance as the representative of the majority of employees. The company agreed to a union card check by the Pennsylvania State Mediation Service. On November 26, 1963, the union produced 457 signed cards out of an eligible 654 employees and Harwood, less than two years after the Harwood-Weldon merger, agreed to recognize the ACWA as bargaining agent.

Soon after, the union negotiated a one-year contract with the company effective January 1, 1964. Containing the standard provisions of the ACWA cotton garment agreement, it included: increases for hourly workers to bring them up to union scale; some increases for pieceworkers to enable them to earn wages similar to others in organized cotton garment plants; a grievance procedure; job and wage protections such as seniority and share-the-work provisions, reporting pay, and a procedure for contesting new piece rates; employer-paid fringe benefits such as health insurance, pensions, holidays, and vacation; and a union security clause.

The experience of fair bargaining and the resulting contract crystallized the union's favorable attitude. A determined joint effort was launched to wipe the slate clean of past troubles and to start a fresh relationship with the new ownership.

Several specific steps were taken. After the union contract was signed, a general meeting was attended by officials of the Shirt Workers Joint Board, the union's plant committee, supervisors, and management. The discussion was frank and friendly as they sought the basis for a cooperative relationship and the main interpretations of the contract provisions were explained. Other cooperative activities, such as joint problem-solving and in-plant meetings between labor and management, helped develop a harmonious atmosphere.

Union representatives have been outspoken in their favorable reactions to management policies. The problems which have arisen have been worked out in discussions. The union business agent visits the plant about every two weeks to meet with management representatives and iron out any problems.

A top official of the Shirt Workers Joint Board observed: "The whole picture has changed. The people are earning much better and profits are up, too. There is a much lower rate of turnover compared to the past. There is still some problem of changing the attitudes of some of the old corps of management and a hard core of the work force. But the firm lives up to the union agreement, and there is much better democracy on the job in raising complaints and getting answers, explanations and satisfaction."

Union-management cooperation was demonstrated in the case of sleeve-gorer employees in the Williamsport plant. Their earnings were extremely low, although their counterparts in the company's Virginia plant had the highest earnings in that plant. Convinced that it was mainly a matter of attitude, management proposed sending two women employees from the Weldon plant to the Virginia plant to observe operations. They came back seeing the management viewpoint, and the union refrained from pushing for rate increases. Gradually, the piecework production increased, and earnings rose as the message seeped through that higher earnings were possible.

For its part, the union made it clear that it had no intention of interfering with the running of the plant. As one Joint Board official put it, "There was a bit of a surprise on the part of the old-line management people when they saw that the union wasn't an ogre and wasn't going to run the plant." The union stressed its role as the organized representative of the employees in such matters as wages and working conditions. And, finally, the union responded favorably to the Harwood policy of having supervisory and management personnel react in a positive way to the union, its members, and its officials.

One Sunday morning during the 1951 strike, two ACWA organizers were leaving the elevator in the local hotel on their way to early morning duty on the picket line around the plant. A man whom they recognized as a top Weldon executive had made his way past them into the elevator. As the doors were closing, he had pointed at them and said to the elevator operator, "These are my adversaries."

Such a relationship no longer exists in the former Weldon plant.

WELDON AND HARWOOD COMPARED

David G. Bowers*

WHEN THE Survey Research Center was invited to study the Weldon conversion program, there was an agreement with the new ownership to get information immediately on the state of the Weldon organization, before significant changes had taken place. This was thought necessary to allow assessment of later changes, and also to provide information that might be needed by the Weldon people in going about their change. It was agreed, further, that similar information would be sought in Harwood's main plant in Virginia, to provide a comparison useful to Weldon people in understanding their own condition, and also to provide a "control" (an independent comparison over a span of time) that would be useful in evaluating any changes at Weldon.

The methods to be used by the research team would include free access to company records at both Weldon and Harwood, preparation of special records where these seemed necessary, interviews with anyone in the two organizations as needed, and questionnaires to be filled out in both organizations on at least two occasions. The general strategy was to get compar-

---

* Program associate, Center for Research on the Utilization of Scientific Knowledge, of the Institute for Social Research, the University of Michigan.

able information, as objectively as possible, before major change efforts were made, again at some time during the change program, and (if Weldon survived) at some later time. The time schedule for this work was left open, as no one knew how fast or slowly events would unfold. The initial steps were taken in August 1962, a few weeks after the research team had been contacted and seven months after the purchase of Weldon was completed. SRC people visited the two plants and their communities, interviewed a number of people at all levels in the two plant organizations, and had a questionnaire filled out by representative production employees in the two plants (see footnote, page 186).

The Environments

The Weldon plant is in a Pennsylvania "hill town"—actually a sizable industrialized, urbanized community, but one with some of the traditions and physical aspects common to the older Appalachian mountain communities. Harwood's Virginia plant is in a small town, one-third the size of Weldon's, but also a mountain community. Both are centers of political, economic, and transport activities in their respective districts, but the difference in size is significant.

The Weldon community, which had a long industrial history, now has a balanced mix of heavy and light industry in a variety of fields. Weldon employees, for the most part, are city dwellers, raised in an industrial culture, with a variety of potential employers and career lines available to them. The Harwood people live in a community only recently and partially industrialized, with a carry-over of many rural customs and habits, and with Harwood being one of the major local employers. The Weldon town had been the scene of early and militant labor organization, while the Harwood community had experienced recent and relatively peaceful union activity. Despite this, in 1962 Harwood employees were represented by a union, those at Weldon were not; the Weldon management had bitterly and successfully resisted unionization. Weldon drew its employees from a larger population than did Harwood, and its employees were well acclimated to industrial conditions and attitudes. Harwood had a small population to draw from, and one relatively unfamiliar with factory life. Each plant had its own community advantages and disadvantages, and these appear in total to balance out between the two.

The market environments of the two firms were similar in the main but with significant differences. Both firms had experimented with different product lines and both finally had settled principally (but not exclusively) on large-volume production of men's pajamas. They overlapped only slightly in selling markets, for Harwood concentrated on the large chain-store outlets with low- and medium-priced garments, while Weldon concentrated on the prestige stores with higher-priced garments. This market difference made for internal organization differences. Weldon, making a wide variety of styles with accommodation to customers' whims and to style fads, required for success a highly coordinated relationship between sales and production as well as a plant organization geared to small runs of great variety with secondary regard for cost. Harwood, in contrast, working with large, advance, low-margin orders for comparatively stable styles, needed to cut costs to the bone by stabilizing production on a year-round basis, introducing technological improvements whenever possible, and thus providing the best possible value for the money. These market differences were reflected in the relative size of the two marketing organizations and in the complexity of their staffs for order processing and control. While the problems created by their market environments thus differed, they appeared to be about equal in difficulty; however, Harwood met its problems successfully while Weldon had not in recent years.

With respect to age, maturity, and access to technical and financial resources, the two firms did not seem much different. Both plants were about thirty years old, both from time to time had resources for undertaking expansions and new side ventures, and both had access through normal trade channels to the same developments in equipment and work method.

Both were family firms with second generation men in positions of responsibility.

The Employees

One might suspect that much of the difference in performance of the two plants in 1962 arose from the character of their respective labor sources. We made a questionnaire survey in 1962 of a representative sample of production employees in each of the plants. We found no evidence to show that one plant was favored over the other. For example, the level of education was the same in both plants, the "average" employee having started but not finished high school. In both plants, about 80 per cent of the employees were women, and about two-thirds were married. Their family situations did not suggest a greater economic need or motive in one plant than the other. The strength of their desire for getting various benefits from their work seemed about the same in the two plants, except for two matters to be discussed later; for example, they were about equally interested in high pay, in chances to qualify for a better job, in good fringe benefits, in getting along with their supervisors, and other similar matters. They did differ, however, in two aspects of their hopes and desires. The Harwood employees were concerned, less than Weldon employees, about "steady work—no layoffs" (they had just had a year of very stable employment); the Weldon employees, less than those at Harwood, were concerned about "not having to work too hard" (Weldon people at the time in fact were not working very hard and pace was not emphasized).

In two respects, the employee populations differed substantially: The Harwood employees were older than those at Weldon, and they had longer service with their company. The differences were large. Very few Harwood employees had been employed less than two years, compared with a third of the Weldon people. Only a few Harwood people were under 25 years of age while a third of the Weldon people were under 25. We think these differences were a result of the management practices, not of the labor markets. Weldon in 1962 had high turnover, and was not an attractive employer for older, more experienced women in the community. This view is supported by the fact that during the years following 1962, as conditions improved, the Weldon employee population gradually became more like Harwood's in average age and length of service.[1]

The Managers, Supervisors and Staffs

Since the two plants were engaged in very similar work, it is not surprising that their organizational structures were similar. Each had provision for the customary echelons of line supervision and management, and for the various staff services that are commonly found in the industry. In both, the special functions relating to maintenance, cutting, warehousing and shipping, order control and accounts control were organized separately from the main body of assembly and finishing operations. On paper, the two looked alike, but in reality they were very different.

While the total numbers in these positions were about the same in both plants, the proportions were different. Compared with Harwood, Weldon had few people in direct line of operations management. The Weldon supervisory ratio (line supervisors and managers to production workers) was 1:155—an enormous span of control compared to that prevailing in industry. At the same time this condition was not offset, as it may be, by staff strength, for Weldon was deficient in staff services compared with Harwood. Maintenance was relatively undermanned and underbudgeted; two engineers attempted to serve the full range of plant needs; there was no personnel staff service at all, and no qualified person to look after records and data management procedures; Weldon rarely used outside specialist aid while Harwood made consultants of various kinds easily available to their people.

But the total number of management, supervisory, and staff

---

[1] Additional information from this first employee survey, together with an analysis of the subsequent changes, appears in Chapter 14.

people was about the same for the two firms. The totals were balanced because Weldon had, compared with Harwood, larger numbers of people engaged in paperwork and other forms of indirect labor—some of it essential for planning and control, but much of it made necessary because of problems created by an insufficient management. For example, goods were frequently mislabeled; this required not only the work of relabeling but also communications and the keeping of records about the relabeling.

Employee Attitudes

The initial employee survey, in August 1962, gave comparative information about the satisfactions of Weldon and Harwood employees. Some of the results are shown in Figure 5–1. In four of the five areas represented, the proportion of Harwood employees reporting a high level of satisfaction is significantly greater than for Weldon.

The strength of feelings behind these figures is not to be underestimated. It is reflected in a related survey finding that in Weldon, nearly half of the employees were contemplating, if not actively seeking, to quit the company; the comparable figure for Harwood was only 17 per cent.

Supervision on the Floor

The 1962 survey included some questions asking employees to describe the behavior of their own supervisor. These queries were designed in a standardized way to give a score representing the amount of positive leadership provided by the supervisors in each of three different areas: *support* (respectful regard for the subordinates' personal needs and concerns), *goal emphasis* (the extent to which the supervisors do things to stimulate enthusiasm for the goal or the task to be done), and *work facilitation* (the extent to which the supervisors provide the means for getting work done).[2] Other studies have

---

[2] D. G. Bowers and S. E. Seashore, "Predicting Organizational Effectiveness with a Four-Factor Theory of Leadership," *Administrative Science Quarterly*, September 1966, pp. 238–263.

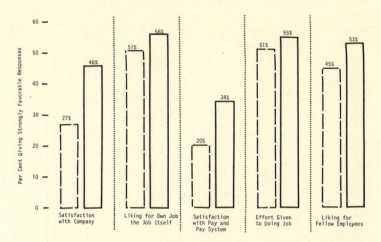

FIGURE 5–1. Employee Satisfactions and Attitudes: Comparison of Weldon and Harwood, August 1962, Before Change Program

NOTE: This chart is based on responses of representative employees in the two plants to an anonymous multiple-choice questionnaire filled out by 143 Weldon employees and 47 Harwood employees in August 1962. Respondents were chosen by sampling the payroll, omitting new employees. (The questionnaires are available through the University of Michigan Survey Research Center, Ann Arbor, Michigan.) Each bar represents the percentage of employees choosing the two most favorable responses of five choices offered, averaged across the set of items.

shown that supervisors who are judged effective by actual results obtained get high scores from their subordinates on all three aspects of their job. In this case, the Harwood supervisors are higher in all three than those at Weldon, although the difference is small in the case of goal emphasis (see Figure 5–2).

Amount and Distribution of Control

One feature of most effective production organizations is that they have a relatively large total amount of control, i.e., purposeful influence on what goes on in the organization, and

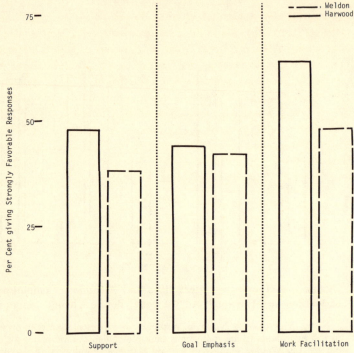

FIGURE 5–2. Leadership Provided by Supervisors: Comparison of Weldon and Harwood, August 1962, Before Change Program

NOTE: This chart is based on responses of representative employees in the two plants to an anonymous multiple-choice questionnaire filled out by 143 employees in Weldon and 47 in Harwood in August 1962. Respondents were chosen by sampling the payroll, omitting new employees. Each bar represents the percentage of employees choosing the two most favorable responses, out of five choices offered, averaged across the set of items.

that this control is spread over several echelons of the organization rather than concentrated in one or two top levels.[3]

Figure 5–3 shows the condition of Weldon and of Harwood as seen by their production employees in mid-1962. The rigid

---

[3] C. G. Smith and A. S. Tannenbaum, "Organizational Control Structure: A Comparative Analysis," *Human Relations*, November 1963, pp. 299–316. Also, A. S. Tannenbaum, *Social Psychology of the Work Organization*, Belmont, Cal., Wadsworth Publishing Co., 1966, pp. 95–100.

centralization of control at Weldon, described in the preceding chapters from the views of visiting Harwood executives, is confirmed by these results. Harwood has more control overall (i.e., more people exercise more effective, purposeful influence on events), and this control is shared more equally among the New York people, the plant management, and the supervisors. Weldon shows a high concentration of control in the plant manager and his immediate staff, almost equal to that of their counterparts at Harwood, coupled with much less control from the marketing people in New York, less from the supervisors, and very little from the production employees.

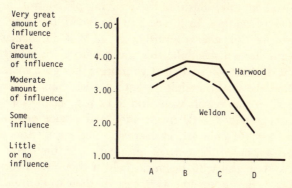

A Owners and New York People
B Plant Manager & Staff
C Supervisors
D Employees

FIGURE 5–3. Amount and Distribution of Organizational Control: Comparison of Weldon and Harwood, August 1962, Before Change Program

NOTE: This chart is based on responses of representative employees in the two plants to an anonymous multiple-choice questionnaire filled out by 143 Weldon employees and 47 Harwood employees. Respondents were chosen by sampling the payrolls, omitting new employees.

These differences illustrate an important but not widely recognized feature of participative management systems. It is seemingly a paradox that Harwood, with more control than Weldon at the top levels, should be the organization that has the greater local operating control. The comparison of

Weldon and Harwood illustrates that there can be, in an absolute quantitative sense, more control by top management while there is at the same time more control also by persons at lower echelons. This can arise where participative practices create additional control at all levels through mutual influence and interaction.

When described in this quantitative and abstract way, the differences in distribution of control between the two plants may seem irrelevant to the realities of daily work in the organization. Behind the figures, however, there were specific and concrete differences in practice, easily observed by the research team members, that illustrate the meaning of "control" in this context. For example, in the case of Harwood, the New York sales people did not arbitrarily, as in Weldon, demand a certain production schedule; this was a matter for conference and joint decision—a participative process that gave *increased* control on the final schedule to *both* parties. Similarly, while Weldon floor supervisors were said to be responsible for costs, they were provided little information and advice on how to control costs; in contrast, at Harwood the supervisors were provided not only with current information on their cost performance, but also with technical help if they asked for it— and a bonus for improvements in costs in their work area. This arrangement increased effective control both by supervisors and by the higher-level management people.

The employees at Weldon were aware of their condition. They knew that their own production work was often confused, disrupted, uncontrolled, apparently guided by malignant forces emanating from New York and by helpful but inadequate forces from an overworked local management.

The Management Systems—Weldon and Harwood

A means for getting a global assessment of an organization's way of working has been developed by Dr. Rensis Likert.[4]

---

[4] R. Likert, *New Patterns of Management*, New York, McGraw-Hill, 1961, pp. 223–233. See also page 215 of this book as well as Likert, *The Human Organization: Its Management and Values*, New York, McGraw-Hill, 1967.

He conceives of four main types of organizations—actually a continuum—ranging from those based on "exploitive-authoritative" principles and assumptions (System 1) to those based on "participative" principles and assumptions (System 4). Intermediate are "benevolent-authoritative" and "consultative" systems. The system that characterizes a particular organization is to be seen not in the personal views or expressed policies of the top men, but in the operating practices of the organization with respect to six classes of organizational problems, namely:

1. Securing positive and relevant motivations from all members
2. Providing necessary communication among members and parts of the organization
3. Providing interaction and mutual influence among people whose activities and values and goals must be compatible or coordinated
4. Providing ways for making decisions
5. Providing ways to set goals, change goals, and evaluate goal progress
6. Providing control over activities

In each of these areas there are operating procedures and resulting conditions that reflect an organization's adherence to one or another of the four basic "systems" of management. Operating procedures are usually consistent in this respect across the six areas, for a "philosophy" of management tends to permeate all aspects of an organization. A short descriptive questionnaire completed by managers and supervisors of an organization, or by other qualified observers, can represent reasonably well the fundamental principles and assumptions that are the basis for activities in the organization.[5]

Figure 5–4 shows in condensed form the comparative condition of the Weldon and Harwood organizations according to confidential ratings from the top executives, managers, and

---

[5] A description of the four "types" of organizations appears in Chapter 15. A full description of the rationale for the instrument can be found in Likert's *New Patterns of Management*, cited earlier.

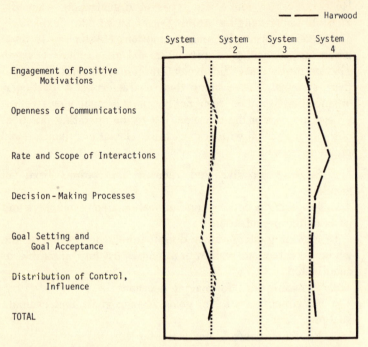

FIGURE 5–4. Operating Characteristics: Harwood and Weldon, 12 Months, 1962

NOTE: The ratings were collected using R. Likert's "Profile of Organizations and Performance Characteristics" (in *New Patterns of Management*, New York, McGraw-Hill, 1961). The instrument consists of 43 items described in terms appropriate to organizations adhering to any of the four managerial systems. Weldon (before acquisition) and Harwood, based upon interviews with Weldon supervisors and managers, questionnaire data, content coding of nondirective interviews, plus observation and rating by Drs. D. G. Bowers and S. E. Seashore.

supervisors of each of the plants, and confirmed by independent ratings by members of the research team based their observations and interviews in the plants.

The Weldon organization shows a consistently authoritarian profile at the borderline between "exploitive" and "benevolent" systems. (Higher-level Weldon managers rated their organization more harshly than did the lower-level supervisors). The

Harwood profile lies at the borderline between the "consulta-tive" and "participative" systems.

A more complete discussion of these profiles—and changes in profile—appear later. At this point I wish only to illustrate the differences between Weldon and Harwood. A few examples from the rating form will suffice:

Weldon people (including those at top-level) say that infor-mation flowing up tends to be restricted and filtered, while Harwood people say that upward-moving information is likely to be accurate.

Weldon people say that their interaction is characterized by condescension by supervisors and fear and caution by lower-level people; Harwood people in contrast say that their inter-actions reflect confidence and trust.

Weldon people say their goals are set by order, usually without discussion, while at Harwood they say goals are set after discussion with subordinates or on some matters by means of group decision.

Weldon people say there is informal organization opposing the goals of the formal organization; at Harwood the informal organization may correspond to the formal organization and in any case it usually supports the goals of the formal organi-zation.

In summary, one can well say that the Harwood organization was explicitly striving toward a participative organizational system and in the view of both members and observers was approaching this goal. The Weldon organization had no ex-plicit formulation of its desired organizational system, but in fact functioned in an authoritative pattern, sometimes frankly exploitative and sometimes more benevolent.

Performance and Results

The differences in performance and results between the Weldon and Harwood organizations can be illustrated very easily. For the year 1962, the first year after acquisition and before change efforts at Weldon began to have a significant

TABLE 5-1

COMPARISON OF ORGANIZATIONAL PERFORMANCE,
WELDON AND HARWOOD, 12 MONTHS, 1962

Area of Performance	WELDON	HARWOOD
Return on investment	−15%	17%
Production efficiency	−11	6
Average earnings above minimum	None	17
Make-up pay to reach minimum	12	2
Average monthly absenteeism	6	3
Average monthly turnover	10	3/4

impact, the Harwood plant was superior to the Weldon organization in every area that was investigated. Some examples are shown in Table 5-1.

Weldon's monthly rate of absenteeism (6 per cent) was twice as high as Harwood's (3 per cent). In terms of operations, the Weldon rate of absenteeism was a serious daily disruption. In a plant of 1,000, an average of 60 absentees meant that the day began in uncertainty followed by confusion as the empty places were located and then filled.

Weldon's monthly rate of turnover was 10 per cent—14 times higher than Harwood's 3/4 per cent. Consequently, time invested in developing employee skills and in gauging individual aptitude was being lost, and supervisors were placed in a position where they did not have dependable manpower resources.

Weldon's make-up pay to build operator earnings to the plant minimum amounted to 12 per cent of its payroll—Harwood's was 2 per cent. The result was that for each $1 million of payroll Weldon had to add $120,000 for nonproductive labor.

Harwood's piece-rate workers had average earnings that were 17 per cent higher than the standard, reflecting their higher individual production. Only a few Weldon workers earned more than the guaranteed minimum wage. The piece rates were comparable.

Harwood's over-all production efficiency was rated as 106 per cent of standard (a conservative estimate), compared to 89 per cent at Weldon. In terms of production, Harwood was getting one-fifth more than "standard" from standing overhead costs that were the same regardless of output. By contrast, Weldon was getting about one-tenth less than could reasonably be expected.

Finally, Harwood was operating on a level that showed a 17 per cent profit on invested capital, while Weldon was showing a loss rate equal to 15 per cent on capital.

A Concluding Note

The aim of this chapter has been to give an overview of the Weldon organization and its performance at the time it was purchased. The strategy of comparing Weldon with Harwood has had two purposes: first, to make our comments about Weldon as specific and concrete as possible by the comparison of two organizations that were functioning very differently even though sharing many basic features such as size, purpose, resources. Second, the comparison will be useful in understanding the remainder of this report, for the Harwood organization became the model for Weldon's change program and also one of the standards by which Weldon's progress would be assessed.

The account, we realize, presents a rather dismal view of Weldon in 1962. There were in fact many things to be viewed critically and with dismay, as the record shows, and it was felt at the time by the research team that the survival of Weldon was by no means certain. The new owners from their background, broader perspective, and experience were more optimistic and, further, were in a position to do something about it. The emphasis on the weakness of Weldon in this chapter faithfully reflects the need in 1962 to locate points of weakness—for these are also points for change and improvement—and to locate the strengths, for these are the starting points for rebuilding an organization. We should not overlook the strengths. Among these were: a plant actually producing products of good quality and in large volume, a roster of desirable customers and firm orders in hand to be filled, and finally, an organization that for all its weakness did include a large number of people with the personal qualities of goodwill, energy, technical competence, readiness to undertake a change program, and a great deal of personal interest in the outcome —since Weldon was their livelihood.

PART II

THE CHANGE PROGRAM AND THE CHANGE AGENTS

Introduction

THE SECOND PART of our report provides an account of the program of change. The third and final part will summarize the results and some interpretations that can be drawn from the events.

The chairman of the board of the Harwood Manufacturing Corporation begins this part with a chapter giving an overview of the change program—with comments about the main elements of the program, their relationships, the time schedule of events, and the sources of help enlisted to make change.

Two chapters follow that focus upon the production system of Weldon and upon the production operators. One of these chapters is by the president of one of the consulting firms engaged to help Weldon revise its work processes and technology of work-flow control, and the other is by a training consultant who undertook to develop Weldon's capacity to implant job skills where they are needed—on the job.

The next pair of chapters, also related ones, deal with the strategies and techniques employed in the effort to convert the Weldon human organization into one capable of cooperatively interdependent relations based upon participative practices. One chapter, by a psychologist-consultant, describes the "opening" of the managerial and supervisory system to innovations in work relationships; the other, by his colleague, also a psychologist, describes the extension of participative and group procedures to the shop floor.

The final chapter, by the Weldon plant manager, tells something about the feelings of supervisors and managers who get caught up by, and become personally responsible for, a major change in organizational functioning.

6

PLANNING THE
CHANGES

Alfred J. Marrow

SOME MONTHS AFTER Harwood acquired Weldon, the need to
introduce a program of continuing improvement became clear.
Heavy losses, haphazard inventory building, excessive costs,
and sagging sales called for organizational changes that would
check declining performance and lessen employee dissatisfaction. The organizational environment, both technical and
social, had to be changed to improve morale, productivity, and
profits.

Interviews with members of the Weldon managerial staff
confirmed the malfunctioning of the organization. Staff members reported that they were confused by the apparent uncertainties and inconsistencies in policy. The manufacturing and
merchandising divisions lacked coordination, and this had
serious consequences on attempts to reduce costs, to lessen
suspicion and antagonism. The attitudes of production workers
were negative, and turnover was extremely high. The preceding chapter has described the extent and depth of the performance deficiencies we found at Weldon, and some of the
organizational characteristics that seemed to us to be the
origin of poor performance.

The central idea we came to was that the improvement of

Weldon's effectiveness as an enterprise would have to rest not only upon some alteration of its business policies, work methods, and work technology, but equally upon the creation of a new climate and style of organizational life for the Weldon people. This view, while no doubt arising from some of my own personal interests and experiences, was substantially confirmed by the results of the first employee attitude survey conducted by the Survey Research Center team. Their investigation, comparing the Weldon plant organization with one of the other Harwood plants, constituted not only an evaluation of Weldon but also a persuasive demonstration of the relevance of attitudes and interpersonal relations to practical business results.

These findings gave us no choice. To protect our investment in Weldon, we had to find ways to get better utilization of the human resources. This would have to be done in some manner that would support, and indeed make possible, the improvements in methods of work that were also essential. It would have to be done, we thought, by the Weldon people themselves with whatever outside help they could and would use.

It would be wrong to say that the change program described in the following pages was planned by Weldon. The Weldon people, while painfully aware of some of their difficulties, had small chance in their experience to learn ways of working together different from the traditional pattern they knew. The general goals of the change program as well as the approach to change were imposed upon Weldon. The details of the program as it developed and, of course, the implementation of it did rest with Weldon people. In the end it became fair to say that they did it themselves, once given the encouragement, the direction, and the means.

We faced some large uncertainties from the start. Could the habits and attitudes of the Weldon people be "unfrozen" so that purposeful changes might come about? Could a rather rapid change be brought about without disruption of the organization—perhaps through wholesale quitting or even sabotage of the program? How could the supervisory staff be brought to assume the risks and responsibilities that lay ahead? Is the practice of participation and trust acceptable to people who had spent their lives at work in an opposite condition?

These uncertainties led us to make the venture a research project as well as a practical effort toward protecting our investment. If it should fail, we wanted to know why. If it should be a success, we wanted to know how the elements in the program worked out, and we wanted to be able to explain events to others who might be faced with similar situations. For these reasons, we invited the Survey Research Center to observe the events as they took place, to record and measure what was done, and to assess the courses of changes as they developed. This work was not, however, to be wholly apart from the change program itself, for we considered that the assessment and reporting of progress, and the analysis of progress with the Weldon people, would itself contribute to the change program. It could do so by providing current diagnostic data, by allowing the illustration of principles and goals in more concrete terms, by providing a relatively neutral source of opinion about various strategies as they came into the program.

The change program had three main defining features: We wanted to retain the existing Weldon personnel if this could be done; we wanted to modernize the physical plant and work methods; we wanted to introduce a new pattern of organizational life emphasizing participative leadership and management. Also, we wanted to accomplish these changes as soon as possible.

The change efforts actually went forward almost continuously from early in the first year, 1962, until the end of 1964, a period of about two and one-half years. The change program was accomplished in three interdependent and overlapping phases. First, we moved to protect the human resources that existed at the Weldon plant. Second, there began an improvement program with respect to the plant facilities and work processes. Third, and overlapping with the preceding phases, was the program to transform the management system and the patterns of interpersonal relations throughout the plant.

Protecting the Human Investment

We started with an initial advantage: Instead of a wholly unpleasant shock, the acquisition was a relief to many of Weldon's staff who had feared the plant might be shut down. Assurances were given that the operation would continue and that no changes in personnel were planned. While serious morale problems remained, the repeated, clear-cut statements of philosophy and intention were welcome news to the staff, even though they were not wholly understood or believed.

As explained earlier, it was first expected that the Weldon plant would, with new ownership and financing, go about the work of improving its technology and cost performance without much intervention except with respect to technical support. It later proved to be necessary to intervene more broadly and strongly, as described in later pages. Meanwhile, the first months provided a time during which the Weldon people could come to accept the idea of new ownership and to become reassured that the hand of the new owners would not be a heavy one. Help was offered and suggestions proposed, but no demands were made. There was no change in the management and supervisory organization. Apprehensions about the new ownership quieted down even though the internal stresses at Weldon continued and even increased. In meetings with the Weldon staff, there were further opportunities to discuss the values and goals that were being advanced.

When the change program was visibly launched, some of the first actions were aimed at problems within the human organization. Plans were made and activated to set up a personnel department and bring in an experienced personnel manager. A survey of employee attitudes was conducted, and all Weldon managers and supervisors were interviewed, with concentration on issues of morale, attitude, interpersonal relations, and motives. Early special investigations, conducted partly by the Weldon people themselves, concerned such problems as turnover and absenteeism.

In a group meeting with a consultant about one year later, the following comment about the first survey was made by a member of the top plant staff:

> It was an early indication, I think, that things were going to be stirred up a bit. . . . I would say it was the first major approach . . . the first indication that there was going to be a completely different approach, at least to personnel, and the attitudes of personnel.

The effect of these events, although not wholly planned from the start, was to get Weldon past a time of potential disruption, to create a receptive rather than hostile relationship between Weldon people and the representatives of the new ownership, and to begin to make concrete the serious concern that existed about the human and organizational issues.

Improving the Plant Facilities and Work System

The basic change in this area was the reorganization of the work flow throughout the plant. Conversion was started during 1962 from a plantwide mixed-batch production system to a "unit system" of production in which similar product lines are segregated into departments ("units") of a size suitable for easy work-flow control and scheduling. Coordinate with this change, orders and delivery promises were altered as possible to allow for longer runs and fewer job changes. Record systems were overhauled or introduced to match this new system and to give current operating information to floor managers and supervisors.

The shipping department was completely changed, with added physical convenience for order pickers, improved records for order control and stock control, and incentive pay for shipping employees. The cutting room was modified somewhat, and work standards established to allow introduction of incentive pay.

Since the clothing industry has hardly been touched by automation or significant new forms of mechanization, the technology of production jobs was left largely unchanged, but performance was radically changed. Some newer machines and work aids were introduced, and maintenance services and supplies were improved.

Although mentioned here only briefly, it will be evident that these changes in the methods of production and control of production work were very extensive. Nearly every job and person in the plant was affected. All these changes took place over a span of about twelve months. They were accompanied by necessary reworking of job specifications, methods, and standards; by the introduction of a special training program for new operators; and by an individualized "earnings development program" for low-earning operators.

Social System Changes

The third phase of the Weldon change program involved major changes in the managerial system and the consequent changes in the social and psychological work environment of the Weldon people. This phase of the program is emphasized in this book, for the reason that it appeared to us the most difficult to accomplish and the most likely source of failure for the whole new venture. The general nature of this phase was committed from the start, but the main contributing activities did not appear until the technical change efforts were well under way.

The central features of this phase were four in number. First, from the start, the consultants' and owners' representatives attempted in their own work to apply the principles of participative management. Second, at a later stage, all plant managers and supervisors were included in a training program designed to bring about by intensive effort a breaking-up of old habits of distrust, secrecy and noncooperation, and to develop openness, trust, and active joint solution of problems. Third, the whole organization, from the plant manager down to the production workers, were taken into an exercise in joint problem-solving through participative methods in groups, with a view toward making such procedures a normal part of the management system of the plant. Finally, there was a concerted effort to distribute responsibility and influence downward in the organization so that every person could have some significant part, however small, in the management of his own work and that of those associated with him.

From previous experience, we recognized that getting employees to participate in decision-making must be gradual. Drastic, sudden shifts toward participation and shared responsibility provoke skepticism and often induce anxiety and uncertainty. Where people have been conditioned to blind obedience and ruled with a heavy hand for long periods, they may interpret any sudden removal of the emphasis on authority as a sign of weakness in the management.

This was dramatized at a new Harwood plant in Puerto Rico. The manager had actively begun to encourage employees to participate in problem-solving meetings. Soon after, the personnel manager noticed a sharp increase in employee turnover. An inquiry revealed that the workers had decided that if management were so "ignorant" that it had to consult its employees, the company was badly managed and would soon fail. So they quit to look for jobs with "well-managed" companies that did not consult their employees but told them what to do.

Furthermore, people long denied involvement and influence in their work at first lack the skills needed for participation. Only slow and careful re-education can change deeply ingrained relations with their supervisors and their work. Workers who have long been treated like children do not, any more than children, grow to maturity in a day. Employees do not learn to work independently by being kept dependent. Only slow and careful re-education can change their habitual relations with their bosses and their work.

The Merchandising Organization

The discussion of our change program so far has referred only to Weldon's manufacturing division. In the merchandising division, located in New York, the situation was quite different. It was initially believed that the merchandising organization was not only technically adequate but well managed, and that it could be left entirely on its own to continue as before. This decision proved almost disastrous. There was no intention of intervening in the merchandising activities except for ordinary management review and advice, and there was accordingly no plan of change. However, the work in improving the plant operations began to reveal serious, concealed difficulties on the sales side. These did not yield to normal suggestions and discussions about coordination of sales with plant capabilities. In the end, a crisis in merchandising made it necessary to intervene and to make changes in that part of Weldon as well. But that is another story. We are here concerned with the plant and its people.

Manning a Change Program

While Weldon had many people of technical competence, it was evident that the changes necessary in the plant called for very substantial help. The changes contemplated would involve heavy demands upon the supervisory and staff people—who were already overworked and short of help. Some of the changes were of kinds wholly outside of the competence and experience of Weldon people, and for these it would be necessary to import talent and manpower.

Some of the added help could be provided by other Harwood plants, but not on any extensive scale. It was thought important that Weldon people should be kept free from any sense of dependence upon other Harwood plants. In addition, these plants had their own problems, and there was no surplus of manhours to be had. Nevertheless, a number of people came on loan for short periods, or to help assess change needs and plans. The Harwood vice president for manufacturing gave a considerable amount of help to the Weldon plant manager.

Five different consulting and service organizations were engaged for extended periods. Two of these worked primarily on engineering and production problems; one team of psychological consultants worked on improving interpersonal relations and on participative problem-solving procedures. A fourth firm was engaged in operator training, and the University of Michigan provided the research team of social psychologists.

Additional talent and manpower came from the Weldon organization itself, for the Weldon staff accepted extended work days for a considerable period, and freed some of the supervisory force (in later stages of the program) by giving additional scope and responsibility to assistant supervisors.

In sum, the Weldon project involved a joint effort of engineers, accountants, psychologists, and other technological consultants. Collectively, they worked for practical answers that would satisfy the profit-conscious executive without neglecting the humanization of management and employee relations.

When the change program began in earnest, during the summer of 1962, it was thought that the technical changes could be accomplished in a year or so but that the conversion of the organization to a radically different model would take considerably longer. As it worked out, we considered the change program to be formally terminated during 1964 when the consultants withdrew, even though change processes continued after that and are still continuing.

Program Summary

Figure 6–1, and the associated Table 6–1, display in brief form the major elements of the Weldon conversion program and their time of occurrence. The following chapters, prepared by the persons most directly involved in planning and guiding these activities, provide details about the conceptual framework in each activity, the surrounding circumstances that influenced the progress of change, and the specific techniques that were called into play.

TABLE 6–1

SUMMARY OF MAJOR ELEMENTS IN WELDON'S
CONVERSION PROGRAM

Acquisition by Harwood	No major intervention was made by the new owners until summer 1962, after events indicated that self-initiated improvement was not likely to occur.
"Unit" system of production	Four semi-autonomous production departments set up, each with a single type of product line and wholly integrated except for cutting, shipping, and central services.
Personnel functions	A personnel manager was added to the staff. Aside from the staff aid thus introduced, his arrival symbolized the serious intent to give high priority to work-related personnel problems.
Attitude surveys	While not primarily active change elements, the surveys and feedback of results affirmed the conversion goals and "philosophy," and aided assessment of issues and progress.
Reorganization of shipping department	A major physical re-arrangement for ease of stocking and order-picking, simplification of order-handling and records.
Incentive pay plan for cutting and shipping departments	Work standards were introduced, with improvement in work methods and reduction of force, increase in earnings.
Management training program and operator problem-solving program	Instruction in management principles and the new management philosophy was incorporated in normal work meetings. Intensive "sensitivity training" sessions were held with all management and supervisory staff and with the marketing staff. Operators and floor supervisors were engaged in group discussion to expose complaints and problems, develop suggestions, and initiate investigation or action.

TABLE 6–1 (Continued)

Vestibule training	An ineffective on-job training program was replaced by a vestibule program for new employees.
Earnings development program	Intensive individual work-study and coaching for all substandard operators; training of floor supervisors in methods study, work simplification, training techniques; gradual shifting of this work from consultant staff to floor supervisors.
Absence and termination policy change	Under new policies, persistent absentees were terminated; operators not responding to the earnings development program were encouraged to leave.
New minimum wage	This increase in federal minimum wage came after the earnings development program "took"; however, a number of employees and those assigned to new jobs benefited from the higher guaranteed income.
Unionization	Peaceful organization of the employees came about (after years of bitter contention); negotiating procedures were introduced and a contract adopted which included improvements in employee earnings and security.

A number of very important elements in the Weldon conversion program are not represented above, as they are not readily identified as separate "programs," or as "events" at a particular time. For example:

1. The total amount of floor supervision was more than doubled, partly by new appointments but mainly by increasing the responsibility and authority of the supervisors;
2. The frequency of problem-solving, coordination, and planning meetings was increased very substantially and at all ranks;
3. Substantial sums were allocated for equipment replacement, improved maintenance: and
4. Record systems were gradually changed to match the unit system of production, to include new kinds of information, and to provide quick feedback to floor supervisors (previous records had been designed mainly for exclusive use by top management).

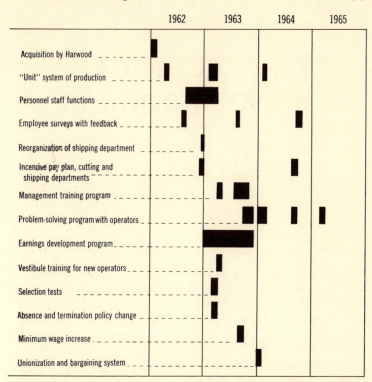

FIGURE 6–1. Major Elements in Weldon's Conversion Program, 1962–65

NOTE: See Table 6–1 for a description of these program elements. The horizontal dotted lines represent the permanent changes and continuing programs. Other elements were one-time events.

7

THE TECHNICAL
CHANGE PROGRAM

———

*Ernest E. Roberts** *

MY FIRM was asked to make a fact-finding survey of the Weldon manufacturing operations and to suggest a program for revitalizing the plant's performance as to the cost and quality of production. Two engineers were given this initial task. Their charge, specifically, was to study the following five areas:

1. What can be done to increase employees' earnings within the piece-rate standards and wage rates prevailing in the industry?

2. What can be done to get a better job of meeting customer demands on both cost and delivery?

3. What plant layout changes are necessary to improve overall plant performance?

4. How adequate is the performance of the supervisory staff, and what is the potential for improvement?

5. What improvements in equipment and work method may aid over-all plant performance?

The preliminary survey and analysis made it apparent that strong action was needed in several areas. Recommendations were prepared and discussed with the new Weldon owners

---

* President, Norris & Elliott, Incorporated, Consulting Engineers.

and with the Weldon plant staff. These recommendations implied a program of work that would deal simultaneously with all of the above five areas; we were asked to carry out the proposed program and agreed to do so.

A fundamental goal was singled out for this work, not to exclude many other lesser goals, but to assure concentration on what was agreed to be the problem of first priority: employee earnings. In a handwork industry, the productivity of individual operators provides a good general index of the effectiveness of the production system as well as of the people themselves. We agreed to the goal of increasing the average performance of operators from approximately 89 per cent of standard (the past years' average) to 117 per cent of standard, without changes in the basic wage rate and without deflating the standards. This goal was reached in just over a year's time.

With this goal, it was essential—and it was one of the most difficult ideas to put across to the plant supervisors—that incentive rates should be viewed as a working tool in management but not as a production panacea. They had to see that incentive pay methods improperly applied and poorly administered create more problems than they solve. An immediate attempt was made to dispel the notion that production and earnings would take care of themselves once correct rates had been established. We worked toward the idea that performance standards, and incentive pay, would have their value not only in motivating the operators but even more in helping supervisors and managers toward effective control of manufacturing costs.

Our preliminary studies had confirmed that the operators were subjected to an abnormal number of job changes each day. In some cases, the frequency of changes ran as high as seven to nine within an eight-hour shift. This was an obvious source of low earnings and high labor costs, as each change wasted time and skill. Make-up pay (i.e., the difference between the amount actually earned on the piece rate and the sum required to meet the plant minimum wage) was taken for granted by the supervisors; they accepted the frequent work changes, as a consequence of management's subordinating production control to sales needs.

The work we undertook with the Weldon people toward their goal took us into various aspects of the Weldon operations. The main program elements included improved production planning and scheduling, introduction of an improved plant layout and work flow, changes in the equipment and methods for many specific production jobs, the adjustment of standards to take account of these changes, training the supervisors in understanding and using work-study methods, and locating and correcting conditions that were keeping the individual operators to substandard production levels.

Work System Changes

Next to the gradual reorientation of the supervisors and managers regarding the use of work standards, our most fundamental changes concerned the broad plan of Weldon's production system.

The task of developing production planning was formidable. Past practice permitted any item to be made anywhere in the sewing rooms in a plantwide mixed-batch system. One effect of this was that the operators had to work on a wide variety of garment styles and materials, with frequent changes in type of work done; this substantially reduced the opportunities for efficiency and skill development and kept individual operator performance unnecessarily low. No realistic, fact-based production planning was done, nor was it thought possible or necessary. Utilization of manpower, materials, and machines was at a low level—a situation reflected in excessive costs for the company and inadequate earnings for the employees.

The improvement of this condition involved, basically, the grouping of production orders in a less random way than was the practice, and the rearrangement of the work flow on the production floor further to simplify the work for individual operators and their supervisors. These changes were not easy to bring about, for they could not be done in isolation from other factors that were at work.

The poor state of production planning, for example, was not simply a matter of incompetence or lack of concern, but arose from Weldon's desire to satisfy their customers, many of whom wanted and got a wide variety of products in small lots with early delivery promises. The pressure of meeting such orders and promises led to putting required lots into production in any part of the plant that became available without much consideration of the over-all effect this had on the work flow. Thus, the correction was only partly within the control of the plant staff, and a full correction depended upon the ability of the sales people in getting better lead time, larger orders for "standard" items, and in setting some reasonable limits on what the customers would be offered. Within the plant, the planning of production was handicapped by an inadequate record system, which in time was improved, and by the absence of any ready means for the floor supervisors to keep the order control people aware of current conditions on the floor. The progress of improvement in production planning accordingly involved a large number of people and many parts of the Weldon organization, and could only be resolved cooperatively. The "technical" problem, basically a simple one, was embedded in a host of complex organizational problems.

The improvement of the plant layout was in some ways a much easier matter, even though it affected a large number of people. The changes involved converting the operations from a plantwide mixed-batch system to one of several separate specialized departments ("units"), each handling a particular limited range of products. Three such units were set up, leaving a fourth to handle the miscellaneous specialty items.[1] Each unit under this arrangement was of a size that conveniently could be managed as a separate activity. Disruptions in one unit could be contained and not allowed to disrupt the whole plant. Each unit was a complete production line except for cutting, warehousing, and shipping, these functions being shared. From a purely work-system view, this arrangement provided for reduction in amount of materials handling, reduc-

---

[1] A fifth unit was set up at a later time.

tion in the number of idle machines and increased use of machines, and allowed the introduction of some work aids that became economical only under the new conditions of producing standard (but different) items in each unit. From the operator's point of view, the unit system allows longer runs and fewer job changes; these permit an operator to develop the skill and practice needed for high earnings. The actual physical changes were relatively easy to carry out, as the floor space was ample and the Weldon staff was familiar with the requirements and methods.

The engineers worked closely with the order control department to maintain proper workloads in the units. Detailed guides were worked out with all levels of supervision in the mechanics of practical routing and dispatching of work. Each supervisor was advised of her responsibilities in the routine handling of the work mix so as to ensure a reasonable balance of flow in all parts of her own area, so that each operator would have a supply of work appropriate to her skill and equipment.

Quite separately from the above work on layout and production control, investigations were made into the cutting room operations and into the warehousing and shipping department. The cutting work was modified somewhat, work standards were introduced, and these provided the men with incentive earnings opportunities. The warehousing and shipping floor arrangement was completely reworked to allow easier order-picking and boxing as well as improved stock control records. These changes allowed better control of stock, and allowed handling of the work with a reduced force.

Job Changes

The reorganization of the plant layout and work flow, coupled with the introduction of some new machines and work aids, resulted in some significant change for most of the individual jobs throughout the plant. Each job change required a review of the job specifications, methods, standards, and rates. This workload, which we shared with the Weldon engineers, came so fast that some had to be put off under a priority arrangement. Fortunately, by the time the main press came on job studies, our training of supervisors in work-study methods had come along far enough so that they could be of substantial help in minimizing and scheduling the demand on the engineer's time.

The actual physical changes in equipment and work methods for specific jobs did not pose much of a problem. Some newer machines were brought in to replace old or outmoded ones, and a number of specialized work aids were made up. Machine-activated thread cutters were put in general use, to reduce the requirements for hand work in finishing. These changes were of fairly standard kinds, not unusual in the industry. Maintenance service and supplies stocks, badly depleted under Weldon's economy efforts, were brought up to requirements.

Earnings Development Program

By July of 1963, three of the planned five "units" had been put into operation. Production control had been improved, work aids largely completed in these units, and rates revised or verified. There was no very apparent reason on the engineering-technical side, yet earnings remained low. This was equally true for Unit III, the first to be activated, which had been in operation for many months. An "earnings development" plan was put into operation.

The immediate aim of this program was to apply concentrated study and individualized help to each operator whose performance and earnings remained below standard. A background aim was to improve the understanding and skill of the floor supervisors in the coordinated use of standards, work-study methods, incentives, and operator coaching for cost control and reduction. Such a program, being costly in staff and supervisory time, cannot be undertaken unless there are substantial gains to be realized; such a program cannot be started effectively until, as at Weldon, the physical improvements and work-production planning are well in hand and the supervisors are reasonably well along in their new understanding of the methods and uses of work study.

The supervisors in selected units were engaged in planning and training for this earnings development program. The technique of periodic follow-up on less effective operators was explained and demonstrated. Instruction included how to observe work being done for discrepancies in method, how to check the operation sheet to assure proper work conditions, how to check time standards, how to calculate earnings, how to demonstrate the difference between deviant and correct work methods, and generally how to encourage operators to improve their performance. This was put into effect in the following way.

First, the engineer made a three- to four-hour production study of the operator to estimate her performance potential. He would sit with the operator and the supervisor for three or four hours, locate with her the ineffective work methods, and encourage her to change to more effective methods. He would assist her to acquire skill in these methods. Coupled with this was patient encouragement of the operator to increase her skill, her effort, and her effectiveness. An operator was helped in this manner until an outcome was apparent, until her earnings increased, or she was deemed unlikely to change. Often he asked the operator and her supervisor into a conference room where he reported on his findings, and then the three discussed how the operator could increase her output. The aim was to encourage the operator to set a small increase as her immediate goal and to make progress in a series of small increments.

This part of the program required daily attention; the time spent by the engineer with the individual supervisors varied from a few minutes a day to hours at a time. Since the aim was to build up the confidence of both the supervisors and the operators, the supervisors were always included in these sessions. Later, the supervisors started working alone with their assistants, and these assistants then worked alone with operators. This replacement of our engineers with the unit supervisor had been our aim from the start. As the technique was absorbed, operator performance improved and production costs began to fall into line.

The operators' reactions to this kind of concentrated individual service and help was generally good from the start. We chose to work first with operators whose performance was very low but whose potential seemed high; this allowed the operators and (most important) the supervisors to see significant improvements from their effort almost right from the start. The basic reason for the dramatic individual gains in performance was that many of the operators—even those who were experienced and skilled—had never before had a chance to discover and try out the optimum methods for doing each task. As time went on, the program was extended to other parts of the Weldon plant, and as work study became a routine part of the supervisors' and assistants' daily work, the requirement of engineering help diminished.

The Management of Technical Change

The activities, goals, and role of the engineering consultants are evident from the preceding pages. It remains, however, to describe the manner of working with the Weldon people, for on this depends the success of an effort of this kind. Even under more ordinary circumstances, changes of the scope we undertook require the cooperation and understanding of all the people involved; in Weldon's case, this requirement was accentuated because so many other change activities were going along at the same time.

The main target for development was the corps of floor supervisors and their assistants; for, in our view, they are the ones who are likely to be the weak link in managing costs. The Weldon supervisors had the advantage of being already familiar with the tasks and equipment involved in making garments. What they lacked was an understanding of the principles and methods of controlling work flow and of the use of work study in keeping operator performance high. At first, the supervisors reacted to the consulting engineers and their training efforts stoically, as if lining up for an inoculation they did not want or need. But time was on the side of the engineers, who remained in the plant for months. After the initial weeks, the supervisors became more open and trusting and less reluctant to discuss solutions to their problems. Though the supervisors disagreed at times with the engineers' instructions, they carried them out, and as the advice was confirmed by successful results, confidence and cooperation increased. Within a reasonable time, the supervisors began to seek out the engineers for assistance as it was needed, and the need diminished.

Training in Work Methods

It was important that the supervisors and assistants should understand the need to have every job set up properly from the standpoint of equipment, method, and materials. The equipment in use was improved so that it was generally satisfactory, and the supervisors easily understood and appreciated these changes. There followed, however, a number of changes in work methods on specific jobs, some arising from the equipment changes and others arising from product changes, new cutting methods, and other sources. All such job changes were accomplished jointly with the supervisors, and this joint work was a significant part of their training. In addition, they were given some formal instruction in elemental time and motion study and methods work.

In some organizations, it is felt that work methods and time standards should be left to the specialists. Our view in the case of Weldon's supervisors was that they needed to have some competence of their own in this area. They needed to be able to evaluate rate complaints by operators when they came up. They needed to be made aware of the tendency of operators inadvertently to introduce methods other than those specified. In the past, at Weldon, little attention was paid to standard job procedures, with the result that on some operations three or more different procedures would be in use for the same task, none of them optimum. Many of the rate complaints and cases of low productivity arose simply from this condition. Our training of supervisors and assistants in methods was to insure that many deviations from specified procedures could be noted and corrected without delay.

Staff Meetings

While much of the training took place on the shop floor, with the engineers working directly with individual supervisors, assistants, and operators, there was a place also for meetings. Group meetings with the supervisors, higher managers, and the engineers were held weekly, on Saturday mornings, from early February, 1963, until May. After an interruption of a few weeks, the meetings were again resumed, as time permitted and as problems demanded. The purpose of the meetings was to review progress, to discuss and agree on priorities and next steps, to get an agreed position on the various issues that came up.

At the early group meetings, the plant manager did most of the talking, with the consulting engineers remaining in the background as resource people. Then, led by the greater openness of one of the supervisors, all the supervisors began to bring up their own specific production problems and their questions about the program as a whole. At first, the questions were directed toward the plant manager, who referred them back to the other supervisors when he could. Later, the supervisors began to address each other directly and to join freely in the discussion, according to the topic and their concern with it. They even challenged the opinions of the higher-level people and of the consultants.

The topics generally arose out of the current operating problems, and included matters of plant layout, methods of operation, labor measurement, quality control, production control, operator instruction, and the like.

The group meetings were slow in gaining momentum because the supervisors hesitated to be openly critical of themselves and of each other. But once the benefits of candor became clear to everyone, the meetings were very productive. On many occasions, one supervisor would present a problem and receive many suggested solutions from the others. The meetings did not begin to generate really constructive thought and innovation on the part of the supervisors until about two months after they were started.

Standards and Piece Rates

With respect to the standards and piece rates themselves, we found in the initial survey that there were some inconsistencies and inequities. While these were few in number and not very significant, they were exaggerated in the minds of the operators who often felt that they were below standard performance because the standards were wrong. In time, as most operators came up to and above standard, they came to feel more confident of the rates and more willing to accept the idea that the main thing, once the impediments to performance were removed, was to follow optimum methods in doing the work. Some operators initially feared that mastery of new work methods might be followed by a rate cut. This was handled by demonstrating that the rates were based on optimum methods, and by careful adherence to the agreed principle that rates should not be changed adversely unless occasioned by a substantial methods change.

By the end of 1963 the great majority of employees felt that management wanted them to improve their production and earnings and that they were prepared to provide a great deal of attention and practical aids in getting their earnings up to the level considered favorable in the community. Their morale improved a great deal, and this helped to speed up the later phases of the earnings development program.

For their part, the engineers had to gain the confidence of the employees without raising rates. This was done by concentrating on the positive points of the Harwood management system and was accomplished mainly through better internal cooperation, control, and communication. Not only were sources of excess labor costs exposed, but such matters as layout, methods, flow of work, and distribution of work were also discussed with supervisors and employees.

Through open discussion of collective shortcomings and

strengths, a sense of team spirit was developed, and changes and corrections were received in an atmosphere of cooperation. This *modus operandi* was applied plantwide to everyone— from the operator at a machine up to and including the plant manager.

8

OPERATOR TRAINING

Charles Brooks[*]

THE MAJOR PROBLEM affecting Weldon's training program, when I came upon the scene in March 1963, was turnover. During the previous year, 1962, 90 per cent of all new employees had left within four months of joining the company. The investment in valuable training time was being largely lost, and at a time when it was essential to build up a skilled work force.

Three factors appeared to be at work, each aggravating the others. Some of the new employees lacked the basic aptitudes and attitudes for skilled work in the garment industry. Others were poorly trained during their early weeks because of turmoil in the factory and consequent lack of attention to their training. The general atmosphere of tension and frustration slowed the rate of learning.

Weldon's hiring system contributed substantially to the conditions I found. Seasonal needs for large numbers of employees had led to the hiring of many people who were clearly unfit for short-run production needs and not promising for longer-run skill development. The screening of candidates was not very effective, and no one had felt much concerned about or responsible for improving the quality of the people taken on.

The turnover rate, and the seasonal expansion of work, led to the assignment of new employees to whatever vacancies

[*] Ladhams Associates, Training Consultants.

existed at the moment. It was not unusual for a new employee to be shifted from one type of work to another several times during her first weeks. This made it difficult for her to make any progress in skill development, dampened the hope of ever reaching a level of performance that would pay off in higher earnings, and led many to despair and quit within a short time.

The problem of morale affected the new employees and also the supervisors and trainers. It is understandable that trainers would feel frustrated with the parade of short-term new girls they had to deal with; and the supervisors—too few in number in any case—were not able to give the attention needed. The records showed clearly that even those trainees who did stay on for an extended period took overly long to reach production standards.

The training problem had been recognized earlier, and steps taken to deal with it. A number of senior operators were taken off their regular production jobs to help with the training of new and transferred operators and with the retraining needed in connection with the materials and style variations called for by the production schedule. At the time of my arrival, there were six such trainers. It was apparent that in spite of their effort and competence, they could not surmount the difficulties of handling training needs on the shop floor under the existing conditions.

It was not surprising, therefore, that the general level of skill in the sewing rooms was considerably below the industry standard. While there were some highly skilled operators turning out a good quantity of first-rate products and earning accordingly, many veteran workers remained at a relatively low level of proficiency and earnings.

The Training Program

Our approach to training reached forward to the initial selection of trainees and followed through to on-the-job training for whatever period was necessary in each case. The program was oriented toward a continuously revised schedule of training requirements derived from the study of production plans and turnover expectancies. The program had the following features:

1. A battery of selection tests was introduced. These simple tests—for manual dexterity, finger dexterity, and vision—were of a kind that could be used by the Weldon personnel staff and easily scored against standards based on experience in similar firms. A cutoff score was set for each test, to eliminate those who would probably be handicapped by lack of aptitude for this type of work.

2. A "vestibule" training area was set up, separate from, but near, the sewing rooms. New employees allocated to simple jobs would continue to be trained as before right in the sewing rooms; those assigned to more difficult operations would start in the training area where there could be maintained an atmosphere designed to encourage learning. Here trainees would be helped to develop confidence as well as skill. After about four weeks "in class," they would be transferred to the production line to work under the supervision of a floor trainer until they reached the standard level of output.

3. Instead of recruiting people on a day-to-day basis and assigning them randomly to jobs, an effort was made to determine in advance the probable number of trainees that each key position would require. New people were assigned to training in a type of task for which their tests showed them to be suited. Every effort was made to assign them after preliminary training only to the jobs for which they were particularly trained. The expected rate of recruitment was placed initially at about 16 new people per week, and plans were made for the training center to have 50 to 60 trainees at any one time.

4. After the "vestibule" program had been established, and as the training workload permitted, low-performing operators would be retrained either on the job itself, under a trainer, or in the training center.

5. Idle machines were moved into the training area as they became available; each trainee moved to the production line along with the machine she was trained on.

6. The training was done on regular production materials and styles, so that the output could be used and the trainees required to meet regular production quality standards while learning.

7. Detailed daily records were kept by each trainee so that progress would be known.

8. The job conditions and work methods were the same as those on the regular production jobs, except for pace and interruptions for personal demonstration and instruction.

9. The trainers—drawn from the regular production staff—were themselves trained in the methods of instruction and the analysis of learning difficulties.

While the need for improving the company's training activities was universally recognized, there was considerable skepticism among some supervisors and trainers about the practicability of the method and of the idea of planning ahead to meet training needs. The new program got under way quietly, in one department where the supervisor had indicated positive interest in the project. The trainers also took well to the new training technique. Within a few weeks the new trainees began to display unusual progress.

The idea of a separate training area proved particularly attractive to both trainees and to instructors, who could concentrate on the task of training without the distractions of the shop itself. But as the size of the training area and the number of trainees increased, certain organizational problems began to arise, stemming from the need for output from each trainee as soon as possible and from the sheer size of an operation handling 50 to 60 trainees.

During the early stages of the program, relationships between the training area and the floor left a good deal to be desired. To help maintain a steady flow of goods and balanced production from the training area to the production line, one broadly skilled service operator had to be assigned full time to the training area. The supervisors could not readily spare the time to keep in close touch with the training program, particularly since they were at that time deeply involved with the engineering consultants on other production problems. Finding additional trainers was another problem, for skilled operators—sorely needed to maintain production—could not readily be released to become trainers. As departments were reorganized, and product runs were completed, there were occasional shortages of work and some trainees were sent home early for lack of work. This had an adverse effect on many of the trainees and was solved by special efforts to anticipate conditions and to keep trainees supplied with work. As operator efficiency and departmental organization improved, these problems diminished.

Adjustments also had to be made in some piece rates, so that trainees working under abnormal conditions would have equal opportunities to meet production targets. Since the supervisors were involved in so many changes and working under a not inconsiderable strain, they could not always adopt the encouraging, understanding attitudes which trainees needed for full success.

Despite these difficulties and problems, the success of the program became obvious to the supervisors as graduates of the training center began to be assigned to their departments. The newly assigned employees developed in stamina and performance. Soon experienced operators also benefited from retraining.

With success, the climate affecting trainers and trainees improved considerably. Most of the operators and supervisors became accustomed to training and recognized its immediate and practical value to themselves and the company. The concrete results are illustrated in these statistics:

1. Labor turnover among new employees decreased substantially. From 90 per cent (within four months) among all new employees in 1962, the percentage that left the company during training was reduced to about 50 per cent.

2. The speed of learning increased strikingly. This was reflected in sharply higher average piece-rate earnings among new employees after the program was introduced as compared

with before. New trainees reached an average level of earnings of 105 per cent of standard after four months compared to the 87 per cent which had been the level for previous trainees.

3. Training costs were reduced in response to the combined effect of reduction in the rate of turnover and increased learning speed. During 1962, the total cost to train one surviving operator amounted to $1,650; by the last quarter of 1963, this amount was reduced to $703.

The training program introduced at Weldon was not merely a project of the personnel department. Every department and nearly every manager was deeply involved in it. The meetings they held together, the joint consultation they inaugurated, and the exchanging of ideas they entered into were determining factors in the success of the whole training program. The general manager held regular informal meetings to review progress and discuss policy matters with trainers, staff, and supervisors in every department. The production manager had daily contact with engineering and personnel, among others, on equipment, transfer of trainees from the training center, and training requirements. The plant engineer had to provide cooperation and assistance in the setting up of the training center, the provision of equipment, and the preparation of work aids. The personnel manager was, of course, intimately involved in the recruitment, selection, and induction of new entrants. Supervisors, too, played major roles, particularly in the discussions held to measure training progress and provide suitable production work for the training center. Occasional formal meetings were held to explain the training program to them, to discuss how to obtain the most value from it, and to deal with specific matters such as the best way to handle unresponsive operators. Engineering consultants also were important, particularly in coordinating the training and industrial engineering activities.

In sum, the training operation served as a microcosm for the whole task of introducing change into the Weldon operation, emphasizing as it did the close cooperation of people from different operations and—perhaps even more important—joint participation in problem-solving at many levels of the company's hierarchy—a process that opened up new avenues by which employees could contribute to their own satisfaction and their company's benefit.

9

BUILDING COOPERATION AND TRUST

*Gilbert David**

IN MAY OF 1963, a direct approach began on the problem of building relationships of cooperation and trust in the Weldon organization. This was about nine months after the conversion program got under way and after a number of elements in the program had been completed or initiated. By this time there were a few—but only a few—signs of improvement. Operator performance was climbing slowly from its lowest level, but remained far below standard. Three of the planned four "units" were in operation, although not yet giving the expected results. A number of improvements in equipment, work flow, order control, and the like were installed or well along in preparation. Still, productivity remained low, costs were high, morale had improved only slightly if at all. For the year's work there was little to show in the over-all performance of the organization.

It was believed at that time that progress potentially available through the various technical improvements was being blocked by the hostilities, suspicions, and fears of the Weldon

---

* Senior partner, Leadership Development Associates, Consulting Psychologists.

managers and supervisors in their work relations with one another. Not that these had become worse, but just that they had not become better. It was felt, further, that these conditions among the higher-level people had their effects among the lower-level supervisors and operators as well. Coordination between the merchandising and manufacturing divisions remained poor and a constant source of difficulty. The plant managers and supervisors clearly were performing at a level well below their capacities. At the same time, important conditions for change had been incorporated in the earlier activities.

At the plant, although less so in the merchandising division, the people had begun to accept the idea that personnel and organizational matters needed their serious attention; this was conveyed in part by discussion and persuasion, but mainly by events they experienced. The first employee attitude survey was reported to them and discussed; the survey results were rather dismaying, and did not indicate what should be done, but did focus attention on a class of problems that had been largely ignored at Weldon. The introduction of a personnel staff function with an experienced personnel manager represented the intention of the new ownership to provide help and guidance. Personnel matters were discussed in staff meetings to an extent not previously known. Supervisors and managers began to get current information concerning turnover, absences, job change rates, and similar matters. Probably most important of all, the various consultants then working in the plant and the occasional visitors from Harwood, showed in their way of working that they considered such matters important. The Weldon people themselves thus had experienced group discussion, consultative procedures, and cooperation in work in ways that were new to them.

A second factor was the growing sense of confidence in the new ownership. The Weldon people had seen evidence of technical competence they respected, and saw the investment of considerable talent and capital toward improving the Weldon plant. They were reassured by being kept on in their jobs, as promised, and by the openness of discussions about plans and problems.

Perhaps these forces would in time have brought about a change in the behavior of the Weldon people. But there was a time pressure, for the financial drain continued, and it was felt that the pace of changes of all kinds could not be sustained without some significant breakthrough in the staff relationships.

Of the alternative approaches that might have been taken, only one was seriously considered. Personal counseling with individual staff members, for example, would have been a time-consuming matter and probably would not easily have dealt with the constraints of a long-established pattern of interpersonal and group relations. Seminars or formal training procedures, valuable though they are for teaching the facts, concepts, and rational tools of behavior analysis, have not been known to produce significant behavior change in the short run, and in any case would take too long. It was agreed to undertake a direct examination by the staff members themselves of their own ideas, attitudes, and practices in management. This would be done in working sessions apart from the normal work situation but clearly focused upon the practical problems arising at work. The aim would be to improve the interpersonal competence of managers, to reduce hostile tensions, to increase awareness of how interaction stress develops in work relations, and to help the staff members learn and try out different and better methods of dealing with their joint responsibilities. It was not expected that perfect harmony could or should be sought, but only that tensions and misunderstandings should be recognized, moderated, and dealt with as joint work problems.

The Training Program

The methods adopted are derived from a general training strategy known as "laboratory training" or "sensitivity training." It is not my intention here to outline the rationale and experience from which this approach to training has been developed, as this will be known to many readers and in any case is available from other sources.[1] The main features of our plan were these:

1. The initial coverage would be limited to the top group of executives and managers in manufacturing and merchandising. Further coverage would depend upon the outcome of the first sessions. It was contemplated, however, that coverage would probably be extended to all supervisors and managers.

2. A "family group" format would be used. That is, the training groups would be formed of people who were related in their normal work and who would bring their regular work roles and relationships into the training sessions. This is probably the most difficult kind of group to engage in such training as the participants may well be reluctant to speak frankly with their superiors, and with colleagues with whom they must have future relations. It was felt, however, that this risk had to be taken as no other format would be likely to affect, in the short run, an internal organizational situation as critical as the one we had to deal with.

3. While it is preferable, generally, to give people the option of attending training sessions, it was felt that in this case of antagonistic attitudes and apprehension a voluntary plan could not be followed. It was indicated simply that staff members were expected to attend. Considerable effort was made to prepare an accepting view; the program was discussed fully with those to be involved, in staff meetings, and each was interviewed by the trainer in advance, partly to provide the trainer with needed organizational and personal background but mainly to explore and moderate apprehensions, expectations, and hopes that individuals might have.

4. Brief sessions were planned—two to four days—rather

---

[1] A. J. Marrow, *Behind the Executive Mask*, New York, American Management Association Press, 1964; L. P. Bradford, J. R. Gibb, and K. D. Benne, *T-Group Theory and Laboratory Method*, New York, John Wiley, 1964; E. H. Schein and W. G. Bennis, *Personal and Organizational Change Through Group Methods: The Laboratory Approach*, New York, John Wiley, 1964.

than the more leisurely and extended sessions that are commonly used. Aside from the pressures of work, which precluded keeping a key group of managers away from the organization for a longer time, it was anticipated that the existing conditions of stress and hostility would favor either early breakdown of this training procedure or else rapid success with it.

5. In addition to the preparatory group discussion and interviewing mentioned above, there would be follow-up procedures as well of a similar kind.

6. Sessions would be held at locations away from the normal work place, with living-in facilities.

7. All sessions would be with the same trainer (myself) in attendance; the new owners of Weldon or their representatives would not attend unless asked by the group.

The First Sessions

The first group selected for training was composed of the five department heads in the New York office, mainly concerned with marketing and administration. Their superior, formerly partner-owner of the firm, was not present. The training period ran from the evening of the first day through noon of the fourth day, and the work was continuous and intensive, with breaks only for meals, brief recreation, and sleep.

The "program" was unstructured at the beginning, as is conventional in this type of training. The first evening discussion began with a problem census, often a rather neutral opening process but in this case one that very soon led to strongly emotional expressions of concern. By the following day the participants had begun to express their feelings toward each other quite directly and frankly, something they had rarely done in their daily work. As the discussion progressed it became easier for them to accept criticism without becoming angry or wanting to strike back. As they began to express long-suppressed hostilities and anxieties the "unfreezing" of old attitudes, old values, and old approaches began. From the second day onward the discussion was spontaneous and uninhibited. From early morning to long past midnight the process of self-examination and confrontation continued. They raised questions they had never felt free to ask before. Politeness and superficiality yielded to openness and emotional expression and then to more objective analysis of themselves and their relationships at work. They faced up to many conflicts and spoke of their differences. There were tense moments, as suspicion, distrust, and personal antagonisms were aired, but most issues were worked out without acrimony.

There was one major problem, unanimously expressed, with which they were unable to deal: This concerned the behavior of the absent superior and his effect on their own behavior. Once it became clear that they would have to discuss him, they proceeded to do so, and with a flood of complaints and critical ideas. Since the group included the son and also the son-in-law of this man, this "breakthrough" seemed and was quite dramatic.

The meetings' consensus was clear: More cooperative relations could be established only if the former partner-owner would work with them as a team instead of playing each against the other; if he would give them greater freedom to act; if he would modify his role as the sole decision-maker; and if he would share information. They felt they could carry on as a responsible, effective team with him only if he would consent to try to change in these ways. They asked if a conference could be set up with their superior together with the two heads of the Harwood organization to discuss the issues openly.

This was agreed to by the Harwood owners, and a plan was made, tentatively, to meet a week later at the same out-of-town retreat. When informed of this plan the former partner-owner announced that he would not attend. The Harwood owners prevailed on him to cooperate. He agreed reluctantly but gave notice that he would come only for one evening session and would leave the following morning.

The five staff men spent the first day of the planned two-day meeting reviewing the issues that they wanted to discuss with the new owners and their superior. Although apprehensive, they did not doubt the necessity of the thing they were doing. At the evening session, the group had the courage for the first time to confront their superior with their feelings and frustrations. They spoke of the misunderstandings that arose because he met with them individually and not as a group. They cited the errors that had been made because of poor communication and of the delays that had occurred because they could not make decisions affecting their own areas of responsibility without his approval.

The former owner's reactions were alternately defensive and aggressive. After some hours of discussion, he said that he had no intention of relinquishing control and that, if he had his way, procedures at the office would continue as in the past. With this statement, he left. Although this became clear only later, this meeting effectively signaled his departure from the company.

The sequel to this meeting with its critical facing of issues was that the new owners and the group members then changed the pattern of organization so that authority and responsibility were distributed among them. They were pleased with this outcome and demonstrated good feeling for each other. They were convinced that they were now in a position to work together effectively, and they set out to do so. The new mood of mutual helpfulness on the job even carried over to new social contacts. There were exchanges of visits in each other's homes, including those of two members who had not spoken to each other for a year except on company matters.

The Second Session

The next group for training was composed of the six top staff members from the plant, including the plant manager but not the former owner-manager, who by this time had become inactive in the daily affairs of the plant. These men had been working long hours under strain because of the upheaval caused by the numerous technological changes and the internal disorganization. This group met for a four-day period in mid-April, about a month after the first group.

The session started badly. Some members of the group had resisted the notion of participating and would have declined had they felt free to do so. Furthermore, the training location turned out to be badly suited to the needs of the group and had to be changed after they had assembled. But once the meetings developed momentum, the group worked through interpersonal difficulties with considerable success. The pattern of their work was similar to that adopted by the earlier group, beginning with a problem census, and moving on to more personal matters of their own relationships and work arrangements, and then to a candid assessment and analysis of their own behavior and the ways they would wish to change.

In this session, it emerged that the problems of the group were to some extent focused, not in the absent owner-manager (as in the case of the earlier group), but in the person of the production manager, who was present. He was enabled by his colleagues to learn a great deal about the inadvertent effects of his behavior, and they in turn came to see his problems and point of view. Subsequently, his changed behavior became a subject for widespread comment at the plant, and a satisfaction to himself.

Another notable development in this session was the beginning of positive relationships with the New York office; this came up because one of those present was the head of the plant branch of the controller's office; this "agent" of New York was, for the first time, welcomed into the fellowship of the production management group and was able to resolve some sources of misunderstanding and suspicion.

The participants were deeply moved by the experience. Several described it later as a re-evaluation of a lifetime of values and beliefs. They had a new feeling of confidence in how to deal with each other and greater knowledge and awareness of their own impact on others. They had learned something, in particular, about the exercise of authority, about group rivalries and the struggle for power, and about new ways to create an atmosphere in which conflicts could be resolved. The session ended with new feelings of self-renewal, a deepened commitment to work cooperatively, and with increased trust.

The Third Session

The Harwood chief executives, informed of the successful experience, suggested that the next major effort should be a joint session for the members of the manufacturing and merchandising divisions. This was a timely move, since the company was about to begin the heavy seasonal production build-up that required close coordination between the two divisions. Accordingly, midway through June, 1963, representatives of both groups, whose duties involved frequent contact, came together for an intergroup training session.

Because all had previously attended a similar session, they could focus on issues of conflict management and teamwork without too much delay. The proceedings were in form much like those described earlier but moved more quickly to the effort to solve specific management problems. By the end of the meetings, they had shared insights into common problems, established a better communication pattern, had resolved many differences, developed some openness and mutual trust, and had worked out a detailed plan for improving cooperation. The participants then and later regarded the sessions as very helpful.

Follow-up

About three months later, in September, a first evaluation was made of the carry-over results of the initial training program for the top factory staff. I interviewed each of the participants. The evaluative comments of all participants were favorable. For example:

> I feel my job is much easier . . . things don't upset me as much as they did before . . . I get more work done . . . I'm not so tense. . . . Before I went to the sensitivity sessions my ulcers had been kicking up . . . knock wood . . . I haven't had a single painful attack since.

I am devoting all my energy to my job instead of half doing it and half fighting others. I don't feel as though someone is looking over my shoulder and cooking up trouble.

I have been given more authority than I had before. . . . There definitely has also been a change in my subordinates. . . . I guess because I have changed toward them, they act differently toward me.

With respect to relationships with their counterparts in the merchandising division, they said:

There is a tremendous improvement in my relationship with the New York people. There is a willingness on their part to try to understand, and if they don't understand, they are willing to say "I don't understand" instead of always criticizing us.

There is a greater effort to cooperate with each other within this group as well as the New York organization. There is a new feeling of teamwork.

We seem to have as many differences, but we straighten them out with less irritation. They even admit reasonably that they made a mistake.

Later Sessions

These six plant managers were asked to decide whether they wanted similar training for others in their organization and, if they did, to suggest how this might be done. In response to their recommendations, additional sessions, similar to those held earlier, were provided for groups of supervisors, assistant supervisors, and senior staff people until all were covered. The membership of these groups was arranged to accommodate production pressures and personal needs of the participants, and they were thus not strictly "family" groups. Without exception, these sessions went well and were vigorous and productive.

The reactions of these supervisors and of others in the plant to this program were sought and recorded on various occasions. I was concerned that the difficult plant situation should not be disturbed more than necessary, and also I wanted to assure if possible that the building of confidence and trust should become a continuing daily process and not just a passing episode without permanent effects. The training process appeared to be, on the whole, more reassuring than disturbing. During the supervisors' sessions a number of spontaneous remarks were made that indicated one basis for their assurance and positive feelings: They had seen positive behavior improvement in their superiors following training. For example:

> There is a remarkable change in them. They have a different attitude toward practically everything. My boss particularly is much calmer, even when something goes wrong. He used to blow his top even when things were normal. . . . It has had a a bigger effect on him than on anyone else.

> They are much easier to talk to. Before, I could not talk to certain people too well. They would get angry or sarcastic. Now they seem much calmer and don't get mad as often, even when something goes wrong.

To get some further evaluation of the reaction to the experience among supervisors, I had interviews individually with all of the participants several weeks after the first of this series of sessions. The following are typical of their comments about the training procedure itself:

> When we first got settled around the table everyone was thinking "What is going to happen now?" I guess we were just scared. By the time we left on Sunday, everyone felt at ease with one another. We all felt we had received tremendous help. This was a valuable experience for me.

> I think each and every one got a different meaning out of it. It's hard to tell another person how you actually feel. It has helped me in my work and in my family.

> You get to see yourself as other people see you. If you don't know that, you can't do anything to change your ways. So I am much more understanding.

Several weeks in advance of one of the later supervisors' sessions, the prospective participants were asked what they had heard and what they expected the sessions to be like. There was more positive curiosity and interest than apprehension. These are some replies:

> I have heard that you learn things about yourself you never knew before and that in many ways you feel like a new person.

> Well, I have heard that they [the sessions] are physically tiring, but that the sessions are so good you don't mind it. From what I heard, I don't think anybody can say they do not need it. I think everybody has a lot to learn.

> I have heard that everyone can benefit, that it is hard to express what you get from it. If it will make as much difference to all of us as it already has in the two people I work with, I think we'll get a lot out of it.

Extension and Reinforcement

There is a possibility in training of this kind that the initial effects, however strong, may remain mainly personal and private, thus not getting translated permanently into the organizational system. For this reason, steps were taken to observe spontaneous changes in interpersonal behavior and, if necessary, to encourage reinforcing experience.

One such reinforcement has already been mentioned, namely, the early transfer of responsibility from the trainer to the plant manager and his staff for deciding about and then planning the training sessions for others in the organization. This was intended, in part, to test the commitment of these people to their new ideas about interpersonal behavior and to make the diffusion of them more nearly a part of the normal organizational processes.

This same group met on several occasions with the trainer to explore ways to try out some new approaches to problem-solving in the plant. A number of suggestions were made and activated. Two will be mentioned here.

The group decided, on the plant manager's initiative, to try out their group skills in dealing with a pressing problem of their own. There were a number of persistent interdepartmental quarrels. The plant manager set up a series of staff meetings modeled on the training session procedures; he asked that, if they could not easily resolve the objective issues on which the quarreling focused (plant operations), then perhaps they should take some time to explore openly the deeper causes of such disputes (interpersonal and intergroup relations) and possible ways to change their approach to solving them. This proved to be a critical test of the training program, for the department heads had reasonable doubts about the sincerity of the plant manager and about his willingness to try out solutions of their own choice rather than, as in the past, imposing his own. The sessions went well, differences were talked out, and some proposed solutions were in fact worked out that then got a fair trial. The effect of this experience was a strong reinforcement of their belief in the practicality of creating improved work relationships purposely and jointly.

A similar procedure was tried out shortly afterward with people at a lower level of the plant organization. In this instance, the focus for the work was among operator trainees and their trainers. The training was not going too well, turnover was high, and there was a prevailing air of frustration and discouragement. Meetings were held with each trainer and her trainees, with full participation encouraged in discussing problems and suggesting solutions. Many of the trainees were at first rather disturbed by their experience of being in conference with higher-rank people, but most responded to the opportunity and made numerous suggestions. Follow-up interviews indicated that there was a positive response among the trainees. Additional supervisors, and also the personnel director, had through this process a chance to try out for themselves the new procedures for dealing with organizational problems. Later, a broadly based, plantwide program of problem-solving sessions was carried out. This derived from the original training sessions with managers and supervisors. The program is described in the following chapter.

One final event will serve to illustrate the manner in which the training program for managers and supervisors came rather soon to influence the course of events in Weldon. This event, extending over several weeks, arose from the old hostility and poor coordination between manufacturing and sales, was aggravated by the reorganization of the marketing division mentioned earlier, and came to a crisis in the seasonal push to build up inventories for fall deliveries.

Three months after the intergroup training session between plant and merchandising people, one of the plant managers made this observation about the merchandising division:

> He [the recently departed merchandising owner-manager] was a very dominating individual. Now that he is gone, his subordinates will soon be demoralized. They are already suffering from a lack of direction. They seem disorganized without their leader to make the decisions. They do not have the knowledge nor skills to do their jobs with competence. They are inexperienced and have had too little technical training for the complex jobs they hold. They leaned on him to stop them from making mistakes. They used to complain he wouldn't give them a chance to do anything. But now that they have the authority, they don't know what to do. They found it easy to complain about his authoritarian tactics, but they didn't realize how much of the risk of mistakes he took off their shoulders.

This was borne out by developments. The department heads had been dependent for too long and the change to greater responsibility and participation was made too rapidly. They concealed their difficulties by reporting that everything was going smoothly, but there were increasing signs of growing confusion. As early as May, when the fall production build-up was beginning, the manufacturing staff warned the new owners that improper planning and scheduling were leading to difficulties. Their predictions proved correct.

A number of avoidable mistakes were made that contributed to the manufacture of a huge volume of inventory for which there were no orders, while the items for which there were orders were not produced. Shipping dates were approaching rapidly, and it became clear that deliveries would be late.

Harwood's top management had been premature in delegating so much authority and responsibility to a merchandising management staff not ready to take over.

Accordingly, the Harwood top management now stepped in, as it became clear that it was necessary to introduce more refined records and higher-level coordination of decision-making. At a meeting between Harwood's top management and the Weldon manufacturing staff, the factory staff reported that the situation required strong leadership from Harwood's management. They explained that they needed more assistance during the transitional period, especially since merchandising errors had created so much confusion. While the manufacturing staff believed they would be ready for more responsibility in a year, their immediate problems were too difficult for their limited experience.

This request for assistance, and the manner in which it came about, reflects the impact of the training program upon the manufacturing organization. They had reached the degree of openness and mutual confidence that left them free to speak frankly of their apprehension about the future, to express their own sense of limitation and need for help, and to act with responsibility in facing up to the issues. Instead of covering up their problems, as happened in the merchandising division, they initiated a collaborative, corrective process. It was the purpose of the training program to encourage such behavior and to impart the understanding and skill that would make it possible.

10

WORK RELATIONS ON THE SHOP FLOOR

Robert F. Pearse[*]

IN ANY PRODUCTION or service firm, particularly one that depends mainly, as Weldon does, on skilled hand work, the attention of management must eventually focus on the shop floor. Here the work gets done, well or badly, at low cost or high. The work processes immediately affecting production employees should be stable, supportive, and orderly and oriented toward joint work goals. The biggest single factor in achieving these conditions is the quality of floor supervision. It is in the relationship between production people and their supervisors that one can see expressed in practical terms the outcome of many managerial policies and programs.

From the beginning of the new ownership at Weldon, the relationship of the hourly worker to the supervisor came under special scrutiny. The situation was not good. Even though the supervisors were technically competent, worked hard, and had many skilled people to work with (along with many unskilled and incompetent people), the work was not going well. As described in other chapters, there were serious difficulties in all parts of the plant in output, work-flow balance, costly errors, hostility, absenteeism and turnover, low individual performance, and accumulating unsolved work problems.

---

[*] Professor of behavioral sciences, Boston University.

It is tempting under such conditions to lay the blame on the persons of the employees or their supervisors. The new owner-ship rejected this view. While there no doubt were some people incapable of doing their work or not willing to make the effort, it was assumed from the start that the fault lay rather in the system of values, assumptions, policies, and rela-tionships that had grown up over the years. The view was that the Weldon people were caught up in an ineffective and rigid "pattern" or "system" of relationships. The "pattern" was internally consistent, evolved in response to past events and conditions, but ineffective and increasingly at odds with pro-duction goals.

Starting with this view, the problem for the new ownership was one of breaking up an established pattern of work-floor relationships and creating one more suited to the work to be done. But how can one break up an established pattern of work relationships? How can one assure that changes will be coherent, self-sustaining, and not disruptive?

Clearly, one cannot approach this in a piecemeal fashion, for the elements that make up such a "pattern of relationships" are interwoven. To change any one part would only disrupt an arrangement that worked, after a fashion, without substi-tuting another more workable arrangement. Specifically, at Weldon, the hiring practices were tied to assumptions about the work flow and schedule; these in turn derived from top-level policies about the development and maintenance of a work force; frequent absenteeism, turnover, and layoff were thus made a built-in part of the pattern; with such a condition of expected change in the work force, the upgrading of opera-tor skills was obviously not worth attempting; with low-skill employees outnumbering the skilled ones, it was necessary to make frequent job reassignments—often several times daily—and this prevented good performance. This imposed limit on performance led to the acceptance of poor performance and low earnings as a normal condition; low earnings aggravated turnover. It is hardly necessary to spell out these linkages in further detail. All the elements were firmly tied together, so that each made sense in relation to the total, even though the total pattern no longer served to get the production work done to anyone's satisfaction.

The new owners, and the various consultants, had a conception about the kind of work relationships they wanted to introduce. Two central ideas provided the approach and means for making the changeover. One was that the supervisors would have to gain a new conception of their own role that included conscious and purposeful review of their work relationships. The other was that any specific changes would have to be initiated by, or at least endorsed by, the supervisors and their people in joint problem-solving efforts. Thus, while a new pattern of relationships was to be imposed upon the Weldon organization, the means for making it a reality had to rest with the people themselves in participative solution of their common problems.

The Weldon Heritage

Weldon had never had an effective personnel staff service, even for such rudimentary functions as hiring, transfer control, training, and record keeping. There was at one time a personnel director, but his services were ineffective. Line supervisors did not support his activities or see them as a help in their problems. The staff program degenerated into an employee information and recreation activity, and was soon abandoned. All that remained at the time of Weldon's purchase was a central service for screening and referral of applicants. Such personnel records as there were came as a by-product of the payroll and production accounting system, and these records were not designed for use by production supervisors and managers.

The result of this was that each supervisor tended to run his or her own personnel affairs on a local basis—hiring from those referred by the employment clerk, evaluating performance according to current needs and experiences, laying off without consideration of plantwide needs, recalling employees without much thought for long-term personnel goals, bargaining in a friendly but competitive way with other supervisors in the transfer and loan of employees. There was a general disregard for the possibility of building a good stable work force, and in any case there was little possibility of doing so under conditions of alternating periods of crisis production and abrupt staff reduction.

Supervisors were permitted to—indeed, had to—modify work standards to get cooperation and production, although subject to some control by the staff engineer. Different units developed some differences in pay scale for similar jobs. Employees sought the more favorable jobs, declined transfer from them even when needed elsewhere. There was resentment over real and imaginary pay discrepancies, and job transfers could not be made on the basis of work needs or skill.

Rehiring of former employees was ragged. When operators were in short supply, almost any former employee would be recalled, regardless of her work record. This practice was supported by the management's belief that it was better in a seasonal industry to overstaff with inefficient people for short service rather than undertake longer-term commitments to a smaller, more stable staff. "No matter how you slice it," said one manager, "in this business if you want production you've got to put on as many operators as you can get hold of during the season and then let them go when the season's over."

Absenteeism and turnover were extremely high, even for an industry generally subject to high staff loss.

Operator training, under these conditions, was badly neglected. New people, and those recalled during seasonal peaks, came at times when the supervisors were too busy for more than rudimentary training; with a layoff certain to come soon, the motivation to teach and to learn was small and short term. There was no central training service.

Weldon's reputation as an employer in the community did not attract the best applicants nor hold the best of those who came except for a few who could join the hard-core group of "old Weldon regulars" who achieved high skill and steady work. One of the consultants, coming to the plant for the first time, asked his taxi driver about Weldon. "It's a sweat shop. They work you like crazy for a couple of weeks and then throw you out."

The supervisors ran their shops from memory and personal observation. They received little information about their performance except on an over-all department basis. When they wanted specific information about an operator's performance or past record, it was hard to get and therefore rarely sought. Few supervisors kept any regular or systematic records of their own except on the current short-run production. This they thought to be quite adequate. "Who needs production reports anyway?" one supervisor asked. "We know how much we turn out and who does the most work." They were apprehensive when the idea of regular and detailed reports was broached, as they saw no use for these except as a threat to themselves and an interference with the running of their own unit. They did not welcome the idea of more record-keeping chores when they saw themselves, quite realistically, as already overburdened.

The personal relationships between floor supervisors and operators were, on the whole, surprisingly good. The supervisors, although usually backed by management in their personnel decisions, needed the goodwill of their people and sought it by being agreeable and accommodating—particularly with the "regulars." The operators, on their side, correctly saw that the floor supervisor was their only buffer against an arbitrary management and their only source for such little help as was to be had. The nonregulars were faced with a system of built-in favoritism, but apparently did not hold the floor supervisors much to blame for this. The floor relationships were all person-to-person; there were few stable work groups, and no thought of getting operator understanding or help in resolving problems of job assignment, work-flow control, coordination between operators, and the like.

These conditions, when described so abruptly, may seem somewhat odd to some readers. To the Weldon people they were considered normal, if not inevitable, and to a large degree they were thought desirable. These conditions are not unusual in this industry; in Weldon they were somewhat exaggerated.

Approach to Change

The rebuilding of shop-floor relationships took place over a period of eighteen months or more. While no formal plan was worked out initially, the efforts did have the coherence imposed by the guiding philosophy of the new owners, and did have elements and phases that can be described. Steps were taken as follows:

1. To draw attention of supervisors and managers to the critical role of shop-floor relationships in aiding or impeding production.

2. To convince them that the "Weldon way" is not the only way and not the best for the future.

3. To provide specific information to clarify the nature and sources of some of the shop-floor problems and to suggest points of action.

4. To provide staff and consultant help to work on these problems.

5. To impose, after discussion and explanation, some policy changes that would force the disruption of the old pattern, thus demanding formation of a new one.

6. To provide reviews of progress and reports on successful solution of first problems tackled.

7. To demonstrate the use of consultative and participative problem-solving methods, and to train the supervisors to use them; this was done first in relatively isolated situations and later diffused to the whole plant.

Nearly everyone in the Weldon organization, as well as the various observers and consultants, were involved in this work. The chief actors, however, were those with special responsibilities and competence in this area. The plant manager took a strong hand when backed by the new owners and the consultants. A new, permanent personnel manager was brought in to set up a central personnel staff function. A special consultant, myself, was assigned the task of developing supervisory skills and diffusing participative practices.

Establishing a Personnel Function

An experienced personnel manager was brought to the Weldon staff in October 1962, ten months after acquisition. His charge was basically to:

1. Take counsel with the plant manager on matters of personnel policy and action.

2. Work with supervisors in solving specific problems of work-floor relationships where these were affecting plant performance.

3. Help provide information and records that would show the location and nature of personnel problems, guide their solution, and reflect any improvements made.

4. Work with consultants and supervisors in setting up joint problem-solving procedures with operators.

5. Improve recruiting and hiring practices.

6. Prepare for, and later help to manage, relations with an employees' union. (It was envisioned this early that the employees probably would choose to be represented by a union.)

The supervisors were for some time skeptical about the usefulness of this new staff person. They were not yet experienced in working with consultants and staff specialists (except in engineering and maintenance); they had no realistic ideas about the changes in personnel practice that would be forthcoming; they were, understandably, worried about interference in their control over their own shops; they knew that some of their practices might well be misunderstood if reviewed critically by an outsider who was not himself an experienced production man. Acceptance came slowly, and only after the supervisors had gone through changes with visibly-good results for their own performance. The acceptance was cemented only in early 1964, when the recognition of a union confronted the supervisors with a situation wholly outside of their own experience.

The Absence Problem

An example is offered here of the application of the change program elements outlined earlier to a specific problem area: absenteeism. The situation in 1962 was that absences ran up to 12 per cent each day. Each absent operator left a gap in the production flow that had to be corrected by revising the production schedule, by transfer of operators from their regular jobs, by allowing work to pile up, by pushing the output of the other operators engaged in the same work, by trying to borrow help from another supervisor. For most supervisors, the first hour of the day was given to sizing up the absences and making whatever makeshift adaptations they could. The effect of the absences upon the unit's output was multiplied far beyond the nominal 12 per cent loss of scheduled work force.

The supervisors believed that their absence rates were normal and unavoidable. They believed that "you can't get people to work on a more consistent basis." They believed that most absences were caused by illness, family problems, difficulty in getting baby-sitters, and other sources outside of their control. They had been encouraged in the past to make do with whatever help they could get each day. The policy of the Weldon company, although tacit, was to carry chronically absent employees on the rolls without penalty, without criticism, without individual investigation of causes.

The information that Weldon's absences ran double those of the industry and of Harwood was interesting but not shocking to the supervisors; it only confirmed their belief that there was a shortage of good people in their community. The suggestion that chronic absentees should not be rehired was not acceptable; an experienced operator, even if not dependable, is better than a new person who has to be trained. The suggestion that individual cases should be investigated was not thought useful; the Weldon supervisors had not yet learned the value of checking their assumptions against the facts, and in any case they were too busy, and there would no doubt be a layoff after the current seasonal rush. In short, the established pattern of assumptions, beliefs, values, work habits, and firm policies was solidly impregnable on the matter of absences.

The issue was forced by several means. One was to carry out some investigations using consultants and staff help rather than the supervisors themselves. An employee questionnaire was reanalyzed to see how absentees' attitudes and personal backgrounds might be different from those of regular attenders. Tables were prepared to show that absenteeism was not distributed broadly over the whole work force, but was heavily concentrated in a relatively few repeaters. Interviews with some chronic absentees, by the new personnel manager, revealed that while out-plant factors did indeed figure in many cases of absence, there were in-plant factors that loomed large and stemmed from work arrangements and relationships within the plant. A detailed investigation of the effects of absences on production and costs was made in one department, and this showed clearly the high and diffused costs of one absence. The issue was included in discussions at staff meetings and in personal contacts between supervisors and others.

In time the supervisors were convinced that a reduction in absenteeism was not only possible, but necessary. They undertook to keep records on absences and to discuss with absentees the reasons for absence and the impact of an absence on the department and on the other operators; they tried to help absentees with outside problems to consider better solutions than just staying away; a new plantwide policy gradually firmed up in discussions with the supervisors, under which chronic absentees would not be recalled after layoff and, after a cutoff date, a certain number of unexcused absences would automatically result in dismissal. Only a handful of employees were actually dismissed under this "hard" policy. The change-over was gradual enough for most to see its reasonableness and to accommodate to it. Many employees were simply not aware that their absences made difficulties for others. Later interviews, which we believe to be candid, indicate that the employees regarded the new policy as a fair one. Absence rates were cut to half their former level, and in the end it was the supervisors and operators who did it.

The reduction of absenteeism by itself would not have had much impact on total plant performance. However, it did ease some of the practical difficulties that were interfering with the work, and it contributed to operator earnings improvement and to the better mutual understanding between supervisors and operators. The supervisors learned that it is not necessary to consider operators as expendable, their behavior unchangeable. The way was opened toward the introduction of broader, more fundamental changes in the role of supervisors in relation to their people.

Joint Problem-Solving Meetings

One of the objectives in the Weldon program was to find ways at the shop-floor level (as at other levels) to engage the people in freer communication about work problems, to create conditions in which understanding and cooperation could grow, and thus to enlarge the contribution of each person to the common task. I should be clear about this: The aim was not communication for its own sake, or understanding merely for good feelings, or a "sense" of participation. Rather there was to be communication so that people could have realistic knowledge of their situation, understanding so that work mistakes would occur less often, participation so that shop-level needs and requirements would be met.

The single most effective technique used was the problem-solving meeting in which supervisors and operators attempted, in group sessions, to uncover their joint work problems and to develop solutions for them. The technique paralleled that already described for supervisors and managers, but was different in form because of the large numbers of people involved. This program was started in October of 1963, nineteen months after acquisition and shortly after the plant supervisors had themselves experienced a more intense version of the program, "sensitivity training." I was engaged, as a consultant and colleague of Dr. David (Chapter 9), to take charge of an effort to carry the ideas of group process, consultation, and participation down to the shop level.

By late 1963 there were a number of factors operating in the Weldon organization that made such a program feasible. Many people in Weldon by this time had personal experience of being included in joint problem-solving related to their work. This had occurred mainly as individual conversations or consultations, but to some extent as informal group discussions. The consultants constantly urged, and practiced themselves, the habit of conferring with supervisors and with operators about problems they were investigating and changes they were proposing. An earnings development program (described elsewhere) had put many production people into interaction with supervisors and consultants in a way that made such encounters not a novelty but a normal event. Many employees had been interviewed, or had filled out a questionnaire, and thus were exposed to a small demonstration that their opinions were valued. The higher-management people had on several occasions exposed their hopes, fears, and plans to a degree that was new to Weldon. In these ways, the stage was set for a more direct effort to develop group processes among operators and to give supervisors additional skill in consultative and participative practices.

A first step was made in a "safe" setting—the training department. A series of meetings was held, each with a job trainer and her operator trainees and an aide who was myself or the personnel manager. These employees in training, many of whom were being retrained for new skills or to upgrade their performance, were urged to discuss their view of their training progress and the causes of their feelings of frustration and discouragement (evident from their poor progress and high rate of quitting). These meetings were a bit awkward, for the new employees especially were ill at ease in the presence of management people, and most had never been in such a group situation before. Nevertheless, they responded with some candid discussion, heard some management views as a group, and actually made a number of practical suggestions that were accepted. During and after this series of meetings, there were reported positive responses, generally, including comments such as these:

> What a welcome change. This is something Weldon never did before. You have a chance to tell them what you think and you feel you're a part of the company. In the past they told you what to do and you did it.

> This is really a switch—to get a chance to express ourselves. Before, if you had a problem and told them about it, they'd just pass it off and forget it.

The idea of a joint problem-solving program was discussed with the production supervisors. The supervisor of Unit III volunteered to have the program started in her area, if her people agreed. They did agree readily, but with some skepticism:

> You mean they are really going to let us talk about what is going on even if we think they are doing things wrong?

The program began with work groups—pressers, for example, or collar setters—who met together in two sixty-minute sessions approximately two weeks apart. These first meetings were rather formal. The production manager, the personnel manager, and each of the two production assistants spoke briefly at the start of each first meeting to outline the ideas about participation and discussion of work problems and to convey their own support for the program. They then left the consultant and the floor supervisor to run the meeting. The operators were simply asked to give whatever ideas they might have for improving unit operations and working conditions. Ideas (often critical) and suggestions were taken down in writing as they came and posted on the meeting room walls. There was discussion of some points to clarify the meaning and get some impressions of differences in view. The resulting list was identified as the product of a given group or team, but no individual employees were identified with specific proposals.

When the next group entered the meeting room, they got

the same introduction as the preceding groups, but were asked to start by reviewing the suggestions of the previous groups. This made for a quicker start of discussion and avoided some duplication of work. One effect of this procedure, both within each group and between succeeding groups, was to draw attention to the fact that many beliefs and perceptions were shared, others were not. The discussions did much to create a climate of openness and trust among the employees.

The second round of meetings, about two weeks later, took a somewhat different form and tone. The groups reviewed the product of the previous meetings and began to sort out the more practical suggestions and opinions from the others—that is, they became critics and judges of their own suggestions. In these meetings, there developed spontaneously, or with the consultant's urging, a number of deeper and more feeling-laden conflict issues. They began to talk about interpersonal and teamwork problems within their own groups that they could do something about themselves without having to turn to their supervisors. A good many problems stemmed not from management but from their own relations with each other.

The problem-solving sessions resulted in summary lists of problems which then became the basis for follow-up investigations and later less formal meetings with the employee groups concerned with various specific points. The employees found that their ideas had indeed been accepted and treated with respect. The supervisor of Unit III observed that two important changes had been brought about: First, the atmosphere of joint problem-solving had begun to carry over into the daily work, and the amount of bickering, blaming, and excusing diminished; second, the supervisor found herself spending a lot of time following up on the problem lists and began, perforce, to delegate more and more daily operating responsibility to her two assistants, who took up and performed well responsibilities beyond those that had ever been allowed.

> I began to think about the problems my unit faced and I began to come up with some answers. I amazed even myself, because there was never any time, before, to do anything but go from one crisis in the sewing room to another.

A significant event during this period revolved around Unit III's use of quality control reports. These reports detailed periodically the amount and sources of rework costs, make-up pay, and the like, and had been introduced in connection with the earnings development program described elsewhere. Operators had viewed these reports as "having the long, bony finger pointed at us"—but nobody raised the issue until the problem-solving sessions were being held. They were concerned that these reports would be used as sources for reprimand or punishment. As the climate of open discussion came about, it was possible to discuss the meaning and uses of these quality control reports.

This was a genuine breakthrough, for it demonstrated that the policy of discussing interpersonal as well as production problems was beginning to pay dividends. The operators were no longer afraid to speak their minds; when they did sound off, it was within the framework of an open exchange aimed not at merely letting off steam but at getting down to cases. Thus, when the supervisors encouraged the operators to look at the reports from the point of view of the advantages they offered, there began to develop an understanding of the idea that a report showing a unit was high in repairs and make-up time, for example, was not an indictment of inefficiency but a guide to improved effectiveness.

As team spirit and unit pride continued to develop, and as hourly employees saw their supervisors seek to put into effect recommendations the operators themselves had made, individual as well as team responsibility for improving work results increased significantly. In some cases, hourly employees not only set new group standards and work norms but also succeeded in improving over-all functional-unit productivity through informal social control of their fellow team members who had not been living up to the new standards.

Analysis of unit productivity six months to a year after the supervisor launched the first joint problem-solving session reveals the extent to which changes in group morale had made for greater output. It is important to remember that at this time Unit III was in many ways an "experimental unit"—that is, new sewing operations and new materials were frequently tried out first in this unit. As a consequence, the individual operators had to cope with many more changes than did those in other units. Their ability to maintain production levels is even more impressive in the light of the additional burden on them.

Diffusion of the Program

The new spirit of cooperation began to spread throughout the plant in a number of interesting ways. As Unit III employees were routinely reassigned to other units they took with them a new set of expectations about working with their new supervisors. Shortly after the initial program in Unit III, the same kind of joint problem-solving sessions were launched in Unit IV, and later the program was extended to other parts of the plant.

One of the main contributions of this program to Weldon lay in its impact upon the conception of the supervisor's job. We have mentioned how the supervisor of Unit III was forced to allocate more operating responsibility to her assistants in order to attend herself to more basic problems of her unit. A further test of this marked shift in responsibilities came about in the following way.

Shortly after the problem-solving sessions ended in Unit III and began in Unit IV, the supervisor of Unit III was transferred to Unit IV. This change was to meet operating needs and had no intended connection with the problem-solving program. However, when taking over this new assignment, in a unit already performing rather well, she had an opportunity to try out on her own the arrangement that had been forced upon her by temporary circumstances in her previous job. With the counsel of the personnel manager and the consultant, she began her new work in her new manner—by taking up for herself the handling of the complex issues raised by the problem-solving sessions of Unit IV and leaving to the assistants, with her counsel, the management of the daily work on the shop floor. Instead of spending her day in detailed supervision of the work, she found herself interpreting over-all unit work load and performance, diagnosing work-flow problems with employees, helping to set subgroup work and quality controls, advising her assistants. This proved successful and was widely discussed throughout the plant. It was an example that broke the pattern of the old authority-dependence relationship between ranks in the Weldon organization; it provided an example of the translation of the new management "philosophy" and the insights from the supervisory training program ("sensitivity training") into a new pattern of work relationships on the shop floor.

Many changes instituted as a result of the first round of problem-solving sessions were at first regarded with distrust by both employees and middle-level management. The idea behind the sessions represented a complete departure from the old Weldon management's practice and a critical test of the new approach to management. While some significant "breakthroughs" have been mentioned, the main feature of the program was the patient and persistent effort by many people. It was not until there was a feedback from the production ranks and the new level of first-line supervisors through the joint problem-solving program that the "new philosophy" of Weldon's management began with certainty to pay off in increased employee participation and satisfaction.

Gradually, the old caution about giving information and responsibility to subordinates gave way to the realization that an open exchange of ideas about ways to solve production problems would benefit everyone. The process came about at a different pace at different levels and in different parts of the production organization, and is probably still incomplete. But the change was there, and it worked.

An Example of Consultative Management

What specific role did the joint problem-solving program play in raising output in the sewing room? It is probably impossible to isolate the benefits flowing particularly from this approach, but some idea of its usefulness can be seen in the way in which a serious threat to continued progress was faced and coped with early in 1964.

An inventory imbalance during this period (arising from a major reorganization in the sales department) made it necessary to cut back production from January to June 1964. Recalling that short-time work had been a chronic problem at the Weldon plant—a problem that made for persistent anxiety among hourly employees—management's fears of a crisis in Weldon labor relations were deep and understandable. Just as the new management philosophy was beginning to build up a much-needed fund of support and trust among production workers, a mass layoff situation was developing. Just as their new motivation was leading them to higher production levels, operators faced a work layoff that they might quite naturally trace to their own improved performance. Yet there was no way to avoid the problem or solve it except by cutting back production.

It seems reasonable to assume, based on previous practice, that the former Weldon management would have solved the problem by large-scale summary layoffs with neither advance warning nor explanation. The new management's way of dealing with the problem was different. First, the plant manager himself took the problems directly to the sewing machine operators, meeting with them in small work groups, generally unit by unit, to explain the situation by sharing the facts with them, answering all their questions fully, and encouraging free expression of their reactions to the bad news. At the same time, he was able to convince the operators of management's basic good faith by offering a reduced work week to the entire production force as an alternative to large-scale layoffs, while keeping a few workers on a full work week.

In these face-to-face meetings, which were held on company time, the pros and cons of each approach were fully explored by the employees and the plant manager. The final decision— to reduce the work week for all employees—was mutually agreed on as the most equitable solution to an unfortunate situation. (The idea of sharing the limited available work itself may have become acceptable in the atmosphere of cooperative group action which the new management philosophy had already helped to create.)

From the standpoint of salvaging gains in operator morale which had been made up to that point, the idea of a short work week was undoubtedly the most logical recommendation. More important in winning acceptance of the idea than its own basic merit, however, was the open and candid way in which the plant manager presented the issues and problems to the employees in small group discussions, and modified his plan to meet their reasonable preferences.

Some General Observations

Several generalizations can be made about Weldon's experiences with joint problem-solving:

1. Initial reactions tended to be hostile and skeptical, but repeated and patient effort by line supervisors temperamentally and technically qualified to follow through on such programs was able to turn hostility into work-oriented, constructive criticism.

2. Thus some of the early group recommendations reflected frustration and hostility directed at the most visible part of management—their immediate supervisors. Later group problem-solving sessions, however, generated mature criticism and creative ideas by many individual hourly employees aimed at improving performance within their functional work teams.

3. Supervisors—even those most skeptical of the whole idea —could be taught new techniques of supervisory leadership, resulting not only in production gains but also in increased self-assurance and security.

4. Once a unit was able to evaluate on-the-job problems from what might be called a work-oriented perspective (for example, the idea that unnecessary absenteeism affected both hourly employees *and* management), the group itself tended to exercise responsibility for dealing with the problem.

5. Joint problem-solving meetings at which attendance was voluntary were boycotted by some employees at first. But when

other members of their work group showed enthusiasm and confidence in the process, those who had been absent readily elected to join in group efforts.

6. Better earnings for some operators inspired others to take a greater interest in job efficiency and to raise their own sights regarding the amount they could earn.

7. Individual operators learned to accept the idea of teamwork production and were able to give up the habits of competition with their bench mates (such as the hoarding of easy or lucrative piecework)—but only when the over-all organizational climate supported their new behavior. A new sense of personal worth grew out of the development of genuine production goals, and these goals were enthusiastically worked for by those who had played a role in setting them.

11

MANAGERS AND SUPERVISORS IN A CHANGING ENVIRONMENT

*John F. Smith**

THREE MAIN FACTORS affected the reactions of the Weldon managerial staff to the take-over by Harwood and to the program of change that began shortly thereafter.

First, Weldon had a policy of guarding closely information about future plans. Only those in top echelons were ever alerted to impending events—and then only just before the events occurred. Lower-level managers, floor supervisors, and employees were ordinarily given no advance notice about decisions to expand or contract volume, to close plants, to alter the organization or the operations.

Second, the company's economic decline was apparent to the top staff, and probably noted by others as well. Those not directly informed by their own work had, in any case, experienced increasing difficulties in managing and supervising the work under the conditions that existed. Some factors that led to this decline were readily apparent: for example, the con-

---

* Plant manager, the Weldon company.

tinuing poor coordination between sales and manufacturing. Other reasons for the decline were not so obvious. Within the plant, which was my responsibility as to day-to-day operations, there was among managers and supervisors an acute awareness of worsening conditions without much sense of opportunity or personal responsibility to do anything about it.

Third, job security was all but unknown, not only for rank-and-file employees, but also for supervisors and managers. Only a few top people in the plant felt secure in their positions and in their economic fate. For the others, uncertainty was the normal condition, and many of them had never known any other condition except during periods of increasing production volume, when pressure replaced insecurity.

The news that the Weldon company had been sold to its major competitor thus produced mixed reactions. To most, it came as a complete surprise. To some it came as a shock, for they had great loyalty and commitment to Weldon and had not imagined such an event. To others it came as something of a relief, for they had feared that the plant would close down entirely, and the purchase opened the hope for continued operation. For all, the sense of anxiety and uncertainty was heightened.

To a considerable extent, the worry and fear among Weldon's staff were related to the amount of contact individuals had with Harwood people during the "exchange" visits that took place during the period prior to acquisition. Those who had come to know the Harwood people were somewhat reassured. Reactions were, of course, affected by personality differences and by identification with the old ownership. Nevertheless, all shared a concern for the future, which now contained an additional uncertain factor, but which at least was free from certain decline and held the opportunity for improvement.

Because acquisitions often result in "cleaning house," anxiety about wholesale staff dismissals receded slowly, ultimately disappearing only after repeated contact with the people representing the new ownership and exposure to their approach. Yet anxiety died slowly. One executive told me later:

> It seemed to me there was no change for a long time. After all the talk about new people and new ideas nothing happened. More than once I said to myself, "You wouldn't even know we had new owners."

The changes introduced by the new ownership were imperceptible at first, but they were there and can be seen in retrospect.

Guiding Principles

Shortly after Harwood took over, one of the top executives came down to the plant from New York. We had a long talk—more than three hours. During our conversation I suggested it might be a good idea if he called together a group of our people and talked to them, since many were concerned about absentee management and they had not seen anyone or anything that spelled different management. I told him it might be a good idea for the employees to meet our new owners and hear about their new ideas on how the company should be run. He listened patiently but then shook his head in disagreement: "That's fine, but I'm afraid that's not the way we want you to run the company. The idea we want to get across to Weldon's employees is that when they think of the boss who's running the show, they think not of New York but of you. They should understand that when they want the final word they get it from you. We won't worry if you make a mistake. We'll work with you and help you when you want our help and advice. But we'll back you up and your word will be what counts, not the word of somebody else from New York."

This view, expressed from the start, was the theme of the relations between the Weldon plant and the new ownership, and was maintained even later when events led to a very active involvement of the new ownership in Weldon affairs. It was the intention that Weldon should continue as an independent division of the Harwood Corporation. It was felt that this required that we local people should, from the start, have both the appearance and the reality of authority, and that confidence in the local management would have to be strong.

The wisdom of this approach was underscored by the employee attitude survey taken soon after Harwood took over. "Compared with other firms," we were told by the results, "Weldon personnel have rather little confidence in the management and in their future with the company. Half of them, in fact, intend to quit."

The understanding we worked out during the early weeks after acquisition was that Weldon would continue with its existing plant staff, and that changes in staff would come only later after we ourselves saw the need for them and had developed plans. At the same time, it was made clear that the new ownership was prepared to provide financial backing for any reasonable improvements in operations that could be put forward, and would aim to supply liberally any technical or managerial aid and consultation that seemed to be needed. They would be there to help us, not to command. They left us at Weldon with the sense that we had a job to do and also the new resources needed to do it. At the same time also, it was made clear that there would have to be some early improvement in plant performance, particularly in unit cost and meeting of delivery schedules. It is difficult to recall now how much of this seemed to be "just talk," and how much "for real," but the intention was given and later realized in fact.

Because technical problems were most apparent and because their solutions seemed most straightforward, attention was drawn first to concrete issues of work process, plant layout, equipment, and method. Harwood had a number of years of experience in adapting to new production systems and could provide suggestions as well as concrete help in improving our operations at Weldon. The Weldon people, for their part, were quite aware of technical difficulties—attributable in part to past reluctance to invest in up-to-date technology—and were receptive to the idea of improvements of this kind.

There was early conversation also about the need to consider some changes in "managerial philosophy"—matters of organization, leadership, supervision and the like. Most Weldon people at that time were quite unable to appreciate these issues, and the serious attempt to deal with them came much later.

Relations Among Weldon Staff

One of the strong advantages within the Weldon staff of managers and supervisors was the prevailing attitude toward expertness and technology. Our people were, first of all, thoroughly experienced in the manufacturing operations themselves and were able to understand and appreciate ideas about improved equipment and work aids. In addition, they were accustomed to having expertness in their superiors and respected it: "I wish I knew as much as _____ has forgotten," one man said about his boss. The habit of accepting authoritative opinions and directives from higher up, while a disadvantage and a problem in some ways, was clearly a help when it came to launching a program of technical changes. The new ownership soon came to share in this respect for expertness—for they were obviously advanced and capable in this way. Also, this habit of accepting expert advice surely helped when consultants appeared in the plant and began their work with the Weldon people. At times, in fact, I think we were all too accepting; we occasionally refrained from raising questions on matters where our knowledge would have been extremely useful.

Another aspect of the relations among the Weldon staff that affected the course of changes under new ownership was the custom of secrecy, the absence of good communications. We did not realize the extent of this until later, when conditions began to change. Communications within the organization—upward and lateral, but particularly downward, communications—were not always frank and honest. In many instances, the real and the apparent reasons for asking subordinates' opinions differed, and people had learned to be guarded in expressing their views. Supervisors and assistants were reluctant to express themselves openly, and hesitated to share information or to coordinate efforts with each other. "_____ was suspicious of me," one of them said later, "and I was afraid to say anything to him." A manager said of a colleague: "His attitude was completely unreasonable, a kind of 'I don't care what you say, it'll be wrong anyway so save your breath' attitude." Another said, "The trouble was, you could never be wrong. You had to be 100 per cent right. You were afraid to come in with the wrong answer because you'd be banged down."

Such an atmosphere of secrecy and poor communication was very difficult to change, for it grew out of long experience and out of distrust. The initial efforts to get free discussion of our problems and to get a freer flow of reactions and ideas did not go well. Our people were not accustomed to meetings, to working things out together, to speaking up about things they did not understand or things that were critical of others. There was not much sense of responsibility for exchanging information and views on work matters—even less for exchanging feelings and opinions about staff relationships and management procedures. This habit of poor communication did not yield to change for a long time, and did not really improve much until the supervisory training program was brought in, more than a year after the change in ownership.

The old Weldon values also restricted change in actions and behavior. In the past, if a person did something well, there was no reaction, but mistakes brought a torrent of criticism. Quite naturally, the typical behavior was to adopt the safest course—to do nothing at all on your own; to work only as directed; to refer all uncertainties upward for decision. The norm was to do no more than you were told to do.

Underneath these points of secrecy, noncommunication, and narrow "minding your own business" was the pattern of authority and responsibility. This kind of conditioning had the effect of inhibiting managers and supervisors from any attempt to expand their roles or to assume greater responsibility. Initial efforts at delegating authority to others were often clumsy: "Go ahead and do it your way, but if it goes wrong, remember that I told you it would." Early attempts at participative and cooperative work relations were often painful and ineffective.

The need, which the new ownership constantly urged upon us, was to see the value of participative management and to begin to act accordingly. But we could not see the value of it until we ourselves experienced it. There had to be an accumulation of experiences. People habituated to receiving detailed orders and unaccustomed to having their opinions sought found themselves in a new situation demanding skills long since atrophied. At the same time, they had to learn the habit of sharing responsibility with subordinates; for underlying the new approach to management we were seeking to bring about was the idea that the most effective use of supervisory and managerial staff lay in pushing decisions to the lowest feasible levels of the organization, and in getting participative responsibility in the lower echelons.

Strategies for Change

The new owners and their representatives, and the consultants who came in later, played a critical part in bringing about the eventual change in the Weldon staff's way of working together. The first direct experiences of the "new" management philosophy were those we had in our own work relationships with them, and this started the accumulation of experience and learning that carried down through the organization. These "outsiders" to the Weldon organization clearly had authority and responsibility; they also had patience and the conviction that persuasion and example would do the job. They were, however, willing to use their authority and did so, firmly, on a number of occasions.

Among the more obvious strategies used were two: meetings and reports. It had not been the usual practice in Weldon to have regular or extended meetings that would bring people together for discussion. There were meetings, of course, but they were ordinarily small, brief, informal, and limited to some specific immediate matter that needed action. One way to break down the individualist and separatist habits was to begin having meetings. These at least would make it possible for Weldon managers and supervisors, if they were willing, to begin to exchange ideas and information. The topics to work on—at first set entirely by higher-level people, but later by anyone—were often chosen specifically to encourage longer-range thought, and to try to deal with fundamental issues rather than exclusively with immediate operations problems. The meetings provided occasions to repeat, examine, and illustrate some of the guiding principles we sought to introduce into Weldon. The habit of conference—whether informally and in small groups on the shop floor, or in more formal settings—gained acceptance gradually, and became an ordinary part of the day's work.

The new ownership began right away the practice of requesting reports or information from the top plant managers. These requests were of kinds that forced giving attention to issues that were thought to be neglected or misunderstood. The same practice was urged in the relations within the plant. In this way, a number of basic Weldon problems were exposed or, more often, illuminated in a new way. It is a way of getting action without imposing a predetermined solution and without violating the principles of delegation and joint problem-solving. It is a procedure that eventually forces one to question habitual attitudes and assumptions, and to respect the value of having a well-informed organization. This approach led the Weldon supervisors to a new awareness of the relationships between their own actions and later consequences. For example, among other things, their attention was in this way drawn to concrete issues of manpower turnover and absenteeism. Their own investigations, in response to requests for information, and the investigations of staff people and consultants, eventually brought about a very substantial improvement. Requests for information about progress of new employees brought about a respect for the cost of training and the gains to be realized by steps to speed the job-learning process. In time, the Weldon people came to see their organization less exclusively as a system for direction of work and more as a system for getting and using information. Continuous feedback of information on progress encouraged the supervisors toward learning from their mistakes and away from fearing arbitrary criticism from others.

Feelings During Change

The process of change was painful at one time or another to each person involved—and all were involved. To members of the upper echelons it was frustrating to hold themselves in check while comparatively unskilled subordinates wrestled with tasks which they themselves were accustomed to doing easily, quickly, and effectively. Until the new arrangements began to work well, there was always the uncertainty about the outcome—for lack of confidence in subordinates is not easy to overcome.

To people farther down the ladder, the regular and frequent contact with higher levels of the organization and with the consultants was at first uncomfortably perceived as threat and surveillance. They had been used to only limited contacts with a few people. Many of us were surprised, however, at the interest generated in the "experiment" of openly trying to change Weldon and at the ease of getting positive results—once they began to come about.

One immediate source of stress should not be overlooked. The change program put very heavy demands upon the managerial and supervisory staff, especially during the months when they had to carry the change program while at the same time keeping up production with the restraints of the old system. The time demands became extreme; fifteen-hour days were common, with additional week-end and take-home work. There were times when there was a real risk of physical exhaustion, with long hours imposed along with the anxieties and uncertainties about the outcome.

Personal Adjustments

On the management level, some who felt at home in the old Weldon system found it very difficult to change. Others went through the motions of accepting the principles and values involved. As of this writing, one senior member of the Weldon plant management has left the organization; some others have made an adjustment that is satisfactory to them and to Weldon but has not affected very much their view of their own role in the organization. To a majority, the change, while strenuous if not painful, has meant a good adjustment to their work for the first time; and they derive from it a great deal of satisfaction. Reported one: "Before, I always felt someone was looking over my shoulder all the time. Now I feel I am able to give all my energy to the job instead of half-doing it. Now that I have a little more authority on certain things I didn't have before, or which maybe I was afraid to use, there's definitely been a change with my subordinates, too. I think that, due to the fact that I have changed, the feeling has gone down through the supervisors." This somewhat obscure and ungrammatical statement contains much of the sense of relief, satisfaction, hope, and task-oriented commitment of energy that was widely experienced in Weldon at all levels.

Looking back, I think the main points in our adjustment to these changes were these: Our reactions were conditioned by our past experiences with a managerial system which had a set of values very different from those being introduced; still the new values were preferred by a great majority, once they understood their practical meaning. The tact of the new ownership in approaching the change was important in avoiding an early crisis of misunderstanding that could have disrupted Weldon; the initial period of relative inactivity and nonintervention now seems an important factor in allowing the later positive change. The changes affected different people in different ways according to their personalities and their roles in the organization. For some the demands for change have been slight; for others the demands were very heavy and difficult. Even though the kind and degree of desired change became clear fairly early in the process, the actual changes took longer than most of us anticipated.

PART III

THE OUTCOME: WELDON, 1964

Introduction

THE INITIAL CHAPTERS of this book described the condition and performance of the Weldon company at the time of its acquisition by Harwood. In Part II, the goals and strategies of a change program were presented, including chapters reflecting the views—sometimes conflicting and often concurring—of some of the key people involved in carrying out the change program. This third and final part turns to the question: "Was the change program successful?"

The answer to this question cannot be given in a brief way, unless a superficial answer is wanted. One brief answer would consist simply in reporting that the Weldon company is still alive, growing, making a satisfactory profit for the owners.

Most managers, however, and most interested behavioral scientists will want to know in greater detail about the outcome of the Weldon change program. Did Weldon succeed equally in all of its many change goals? Did some elements in the change program work out well, others not so well? Were there some side effects, unanticipated, that should be noted? Did some change in attitudes and personal relationships occur, and if they did, is there some evidence about the contribution thus made, or not made, to the improved performance of the firm?

The chapters that follow attempt to deal with queries of these kinds. Chapter 12 details the changed performance of Weldon as an economic unit, and compares Weldon with Harwood. Chapter 13 focuses upon changes in operator performance, and takes up the task of isolating the program elements that had a significant impact on individual work performance. Chapter 14 considers the Weldon program with respect to its goals of improving morale, attitudes, personal relationships. Chapter 15 reviews the evidence concerning the introduction—only partly successful—of a new "philosophy" to guide supervisors and managers.

The final two chapters attempt to evaluate and interpret the Weldon case in two ways. Chapter 16 considers the relationship of the Weldon experience to issues of theory, asking how the evidence at hand strengthens or weakens the plausibility of certain organizational propositions that are currently under dispute. The final chapter, by Dr. Marrow, aims to put the Weldon experience into a broader context of social change and societal adaptation.

12

ORGANIZATIONAL PERFORMANCE

David G. Bowers and Stanley E. Seashore[*]

ASSESSING THE VALUE of a management strategy and philosophy must rest, first, upon the output of the organization and its efficiency in using its resources. What effect did the Weldon change program have upon the global, companywide indicators of performance? This chapter summarizes in concrete terms the changes that took place in Weldon's performance between 1962 and 1964. The basis for measuring change in organizational performance is primarily a comparison between Weldon's own performance in the years 1962 and 1964. In addition, however, since another Harwood plant had been used as a comparison in planning Weldon's change potential, we include in this chapter some comparisons between the Weldon and Harwood plants.[1]

The ownership changed at the start of 1962, but there was no effective change program during that calendar year; performance remained approximately what it was in the preceding

---

[*] Dr. Bowers' identification appears at the beginning of Chapter 5; Stanley E. Seashore, Ph.D., is assistant director of the Institute for Social Research, and professor of psychology, the University of Michigan.

[1] A description of the two plants is given at the beginning of Chapter 5.

year. The year of 1963 was the main period of change: The change activities initiated earlier began to have some effects, and various additional activities were carried out. By the end of 1963 the main period of rapid change in performance was over, and further change settled down to what appears to be, and we expect will be, a "normal" rate of change in over-all organizational functioning.

Although the new Weldon owners held to a number of organizational objectives, our attention here is limited to a few indicators that refer to main goals:

1. Attainment of a reasonably good profit return, instead of a loss, on invested capital.
2. Improvement in operator production efficiency.
3. More economical use of manpower skill resources by avoiding their loss through absence and turnover.

Table 12–1 shows the Weldon change and the Harwood comparison with respect to return on capital investment. Weldon had a loss of 15 per cent on its capitalization during fiscal 1962 and a return of 17 per cent during fiscal 1964. One condition that makes possible such a sharp change in return rate is that apparel manufacturing is a "labor-intensive" industry, with relatively modest capital in relation to total value added to its raw materials. Nevertheless, the improvement is striking and most satisfying. As the figure shows, Weldon in 1964 did almost as well as Harwood by this index, Harwood getting a 21 per cent return.

Production efficiency changed markedly. By fall 1962, Weldon was rated by the engineers at 19 per cent below standard productivity for all production employees combined, (its actual performance for the entire year was slightly higher), in comparison with Harwood's estimated[2] efficiency of 6 per cent above standard for that year. During 1964, Weldon performed at 114 per cent efficiency. During the inter-

---

[2] Estimate based upon data for early 1963; Harwood records were not at that time kept in a form allowing direct computation of production efficiency.

TABLE 12-1

INDICATORS OF ORGANIZATION EFFICIENCY IN PRODUCTION,
HARWOOD AND WELDON, 1962 AND 1964

Area of Performance	YEAR	WELDON	HARWOOD
Return on capital invested	1962	−15%	+17%
	1964	+17	+21
Make-up pay	1962	12	2
	1964	4	2
Production efficiency	1962	−11	6
	1964	+14	16
Earnings above minimum	1962	None	17
(Piece rate and other	1964	16	22
incentive employees only)			
Operator turnover rates	1962	10	3/4
(monthly basis)	1964	4	3/4
Absences from work (daily rate,	1962	6	3
production employees only)	1964	3	3

vening year, Harwood had also improved its efficiency, to 116 per cent of standard.

These changes in operator production efficiency for the period under consideration are represented here by a line graph (Figure 12–1) in order to show in detail the accelerating rate of change during 1963 followed by a further increase at a diminished rate during 1964. The improvement continues through 1964. On an average for the entire year, the performance of Weldon's piece-rate employees against their individual job standard was 89 per cent (i.e., 11 percentage points below standard) in 1962 and rose to 114 per cent by early 1964. While most of the jobs were changed during this period (reorganization of work rooms, new models to produce, new work aids, etc.) the standards for the changed jobs are thought to be entirely comparable to the earlier ones, except in the case of Unit I (the special products unit) in which the

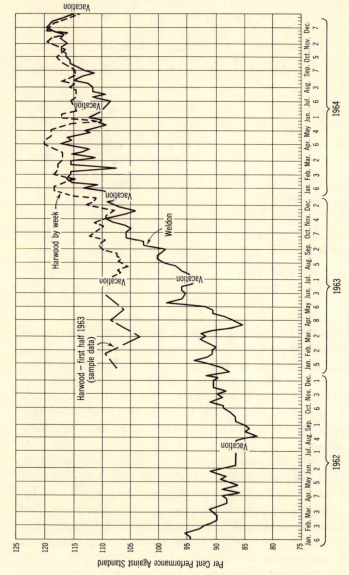

FIGURE 12–1. Comparison of Harwood-Weldon Mean Weekly Operator Performance Against Standard, 1962–64

rate adjustment required by the new work flow was handled by a blanket change rather than by a rate change for each job. The graph shows that operator performance at Harwood during the same period had also improved, and during 1964 was only slightly superior to Weldon's.

One of the high costs incurred by Weldon during and preceding 1962 took the form of make-up pay—i.e., payments made to supplement pay actually earned, in order to satisfy the minimum wage requirement. These supplemental payments during 1962 were a 12 per cent addition to payroll, reflecting the large number of Weldon operators who at that time were performing at levels below standard. During 1964, make-up pay was cut to 4 per cent. During the same period, Harwood remained stable at 2 per cent make-up pay. Weldon's improvement is attributable to several factors in the change program; these are discussed in considerable detail in the next chapter.

Another rather different indicator of organizationwide efficiency in production is the rate of operator earnings for above-standard performance. While make-up pay is a direct cost with no return to the firm's accounts, the earnings over standard represent a gain by getting additional production from a given capital base and with little additional cost except for materials and supplies. For Weldon in 1962, average earned pay, as distinguished from earned pay plus make-up, was almost exactly equal to the guaranteed amount. In 1964, this rose substantially, so that 16 per cent of actual pay was for payments in excess of the guarantee. The change is the combined effect of reduced make-up plus added earnings over standard. Harwood, during the same period, also improved, from 17 per cent to 22 per cent, and thus continued to lead Weldon by this index, as shown in Table 12–1.

Two figures in Table 12–1 represent organization performance in the preservation and utilization of skilled manpower. This form of investment is not ordinarily capitalized in accounts, but nevertheless in a handwork industry it is a large item of potential loss. Weldon's operator termination rate was 10 per cent per month during 1962, dropping to less than half of this during 1964. Harwood meanwhile continued at a stable and very low loss rate of less than 1 per cent. As to daily absences, Weldon improved from 6 per cent to 3 per cent, while Harwood remained steady at about 3 per cent—a level some regard as an optimum for employee convenience and health in the industry.

There are other indicators of organizational performance that might be mentioned here. For example, Weldon's rate of manufacturing defects (those caught and corrected within the plant) was reduced by 39 per cent; this improvement was not a result of slipshod or changing quality inspection standards, for during the same period the rate of customer returns also dropped—and by 57 per cent. But there is little point in repeating the obvious conclusion already made. In all of the indicators examined, Weldon improved between 1962 and 1964, and in all Weldon approached toward the Harwood standard, which itself appears to be a continually rising or optimizing one.

13

OPERATOR PERFORMANCE

David G. Bowers and Stanley E. Seashore

IN THE APPAREL industry, operator performance in relation to productivity standards is one of the best over-all indicators of the combined effects of excellence in management, and of skill and motivation of the operators. Early in the Weldon change program, the goal was set of trying to achieve improved operator performance, with the specific goal of getting the average up to 117 per cent of standard. This goal was reached.

Our aim in this chapter is to examine the course of this improvement from a low point of 81 per cent to a high of 119 per cent (stable low of 89 per cent and stable high of about 114 per cent, still rising), in order to form some conclusions about the relative impact of the various elements in the program.

This analysis focuses, not upon the production system as a whole, but solely upon the productive efficiency of machine operators. If one accepts, as we do, that the net performance of a production *system* (including people, work processes, materials, markets, and so forth) is an amalgam of many interacting forces, then we should expect general changes to conceal the total contribution of any one force. Furthermore, if we expect, as we do, that some program elements are likely to generate immediate effects, while others have their effects only over a longer time span, then we can hardly be confident of being able to separate out the consequences of mixed long-term and short-term program elements.

Within these limitations, it seems useful to attempt to determine the comparative contributions to improved operator performance, during the time of the investigation, of various elements of the change program. Most of these program elements were, after all, definite in purpose and, in themselves, limited in scope. Some notion of their relative, immediate success is essential to an understanding of why operator performance changed so dramatically.

Our conclusion is that four elements in the change program had effects of a size and immediacy such that we could link short-run improvements with the program elements. These are: the earnings development program with operators, the training of staff in interpersonal relations, the training of operators in group problem-solving, and the encouragement of termination for operators whose performance remained persistently low. Other minor and miscellaneous program elements also appeared to have effects, but none that we could identify with confidence.

It should be emphasized that these conclusions are highly speculative, despite the large volume of statistical data we examined with care. A discussion of our doubts regarding the conclusions comes at the end of this chapter.

After some comments, next, about the methods used, this chapter moves on to summarize the operator performance changes we wish to understand, and to a discussion of each program element that might reasonably be thought to have a part in the over-all performance gain.

Analysis Method

The plan of analysis is quite simple. We first plotted the weekly changes in the average performance of operators over a span of time. The data refer to those production employees, a great majority of the total, who actually worked on jobs having predetermined production standards. Similar plots were made separately for each of the four main production units for portions of the time period—e.g., for the year 1963 during which most of the increase in performance took place.

The second step in the analysis was to evaluate the effects on productivity of certain events and conditions that are not a part of the Weldon change program—such factors as vacation shutdowns, seasonal conversion from spring to fall styles and vice versa, and any other disruptions that might conceal systematic improvements arising from the change program itself. After this step, a simplified graph of productivity changes could be made, to show the segments of time during which there occurred definite increases or decreases in productivity that presumably arose from the change program itself.

The third phase of the analysis was to review the changes in productivity together with the sequence of change program events to see if there were any correspondences between them. Some were found. Statistical tests, and more detailed data on some events, were introduced to help assess possible conclusions about effects of specific program elements.

This analysis method, it will be noted, is "loaded" in favor of those program elements that can reasonably be expected to have direct short-run effects on operator performance, and against those that have their effects spread over a longer time.

The Operator Productivity Curves

Figure 12–1 shows the weekly progress of Weldon's improvement in operator productivity, in relation to that of Harwood, for the three-year period January 1962 through December 1964. It shows clearly a decline during 1962 with a partial recovery at the end of that year, followed by an erratic but substantial rise during 1963, and a leveling-off during 1964.

The same data are represented with additional detail in Figure 13–1. This shows the Weldon operator productivity

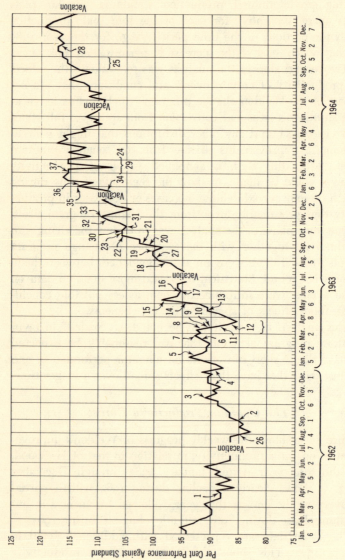

FIGURE 13–1. Weldon: Mean Weekly Operator Performance Against Standard, 1962–64

Key to Figure 13–1

1. Establishment of Unit III, one of four semi-autonomous production departments
2. Personnel manager and second engineer hired
3. Introduction of on-the-job training program
4. Breakdown of on-the-job training program
5. Establishment of production Unit IV
6. Introduction into Unit IV of earnings development program, consisting of intensive training of substandard operators, and of instruction of floor supervisors in more efficient techniques
7. Establishment of production Unit V; Unit I established as consolidation of remainder
8. Earnings development program initiated in Unit I
9. Vision and dexterity tests used in hiring employees
10. Earnings development program terminated in Unit IV
11. Absence policy made more stringent
12. Establishment of training center
13. Plant top management engage in "sensitivity training" seminars
14. 15 per cent bonus plan introduced in Unit I
15. Earnings development program starts for the first time in Unit V
16. Earnings development program terminated in Unit V temporarily; engineers withdrawn from Unit V for work in Unit III
17. Earnings development program introduced in Unit III
18. Earnings development program terminated in Unit I
19. First group of supervisors participates in "sensitivity training" seminar
20. Increase in federal minimum wage
21. Second group of supervisors participates in "sensitivity training" seminar
22. Third group of supervisors participates in "sensitivity training" seminar
23. Earnings development program terminated in Unit III
24. Introduction of work standards and incentive pay program in cutting department
25. Incentive pay program initiated in shipping department
26. Institute for Social Research administers questionnaire, July 31, 1962
27. Questionnaire administration, August 1, 1963

28. Questionnaire administration, October 26–27, 1964
29. Physical rearrangement and reorganization of shipping department
30. Earnings development program initiated in Unit V for the second time
31. Group problem-solving introduced in Unit III
32. Follow-up of group problem-solving in Unit III
33. Earnings development program terminated in Unit V
34. Establishment of Unit II
35. Unionization
36. Group problem-solving introduced in Unit IV
37. Follow-up of group problem-solving in Unit IV

curve together with the series of events that need to be examined in order to understand the changes that occur. The main part of this chapter is an interpretation of this curve.

A third representation of Weldon's operator productivity improvement appears in Figure 13–2. The background is the basic weekly data shown in other figures, but on this we have superimposed heavy lines representing the main distinctive phases of change we wish to account for. Each "phase" is a period of steady change separated from the succeeding phase by either an interrupting event or by a distinct change in the slope of the curve. It is apparent from this figure that there were indeed phases of change, with some rather abrupt interruptions and alternations in slope in the course of an underlying rise in performance.

"Background" Events

Before getting down to the change program elements we wish to examine, one further preparatory step is needed. This is to note certain factors that affect the operator productivity curve but are of no interest in our analysis.[1]

The main factor of this kind is the periodic occurrence of vacations. Weldon has the custom of closing the plant for a vacation period in early July of each year, and these closings are indicated on Figure 13–1, along with a supplemental vaca-

---

[1] The casual reader may wish to skip to page 167, where the main change program elements are discussed.

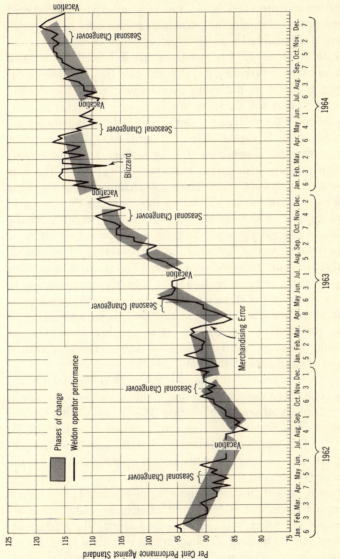

FIGURE 13–2. Weldon: Phases of Change in Operator Performance Against Standard, 1962–64

tion closedown at Christmas time in 1963. All of the four vacations are preceded by a drop in productivity, occasioned by disruption of production schedules preparatory to the close-down, and possibly by an anticipatory mood of change among operators. Three of the vacations are followed by a brief recovery rise in productivity, the odd case being in July 1962, during a phase of declining productivity when the decline continued after the vacation break.

A second type of "background" event is the seasonal change-over from fall to spring styles (in April–May) of each year, and a reverse changeover in November. Each "seasonal" change involves changes in materials as well as in the jobs associated with each style. These job changes are of the same kind as those occurring all during the year, but they occur in great number at changeover time. Each job change normally depresses an operator's productivity for a period of a day or so to several weeks, so we expect a lowering of plantwide productivity at such seasonal times, unless there are other counteracting forces. Figure 13–1 shows the expected dip in productivity for the three occasions after mid-1963. Two occasions in 1962 do not show the dip, but these were at times when productivity was already at a very low level. The remaining occasion, in the spring of 1963, coincides with a period of disruption in the plant, and the effect of the seasonal changeover is concealed behind other more potent forces.

Beyond these expected seasonal declines, however, there is one unusually sharp drop, during March 1963. This decline resulted from a merchandising error. Although both Units III and IV had been established to handle long-run "simple" product lines, an overcommitment to surplice garments by the sales force required the assignment of the work forces of those two units, in part, to make the oversold items. This seriously disrupted a rising trend in productivity, as many operators were put on unfamiliar and undesired work. The other units showed relatively small declines at this disturbed time.

One other "background" factor can be noted briefly. There is a sharp drop and recovery in productivity in late February 1964. The explanation is simple: A blizzard disrupted production for several days, and those operators who did come to work could not be used on their regular jobs.

Change Events and Programs

The various events and activities in the Weldon program have been described in the previous chapters. Some of them, including those that are perhaps most fundamental, are of a general kind that cannot be said to occur at a particular time nor to involve specific identifiable persons. For example, the increase in total amount of supervision was spread over the entire period from the fall of 1962 through 1963, and cannot be pinned down as an "event" or a "program." Similarly, the efforts of the new ownership and later of the Weldon top management to advocate a new philosophy of management to Weldon people were gradual over a period of two years. Such factors in Weldon's productivity improvement no doubt had some effects, but they cannot be isolated by our analysis method and are omitted from this analysis. The specific events we do consider are listed in Table 13–1, roughly in the order of their initial time of occurrence.

TABLE 13–1

WELDON CHANGE EVENTS AND PROGRAMS IN ORDER OF THEIR OCCURRENCE

Conversion to a Unit System of Production with Improved Production Planning
One of the basic changes, already described in detail, was the conversion of plant layout from functional separation (coats, trousers, pressing) to a system of product-style units handling the production of coats and trousers and the pressing and boxing of garments. Various styles of garments were extracted from the original processing system at particular times, leaving a "residue" unit handling speciality items.

Attitude Surveys Among Production Employees
Questionnaire measurements of organizational variables were obtained in 1962, 1963, and 1964.

TABLE 13–1 (Continued)

Enlargement of Weldon's Permanent Professional Staff by Addition of a Personnel Director and a Second Engineer
During 1962 a personnel manager and a second engineer were hired.

Reorganization of the Shipping Room
The work layout of the shipping room was completely changed to make it easier to locate stock and process orders.

Introduction of Incentive Pay for Cutting and Shipping
Prior to the acquisition, employees in the cutting and shipping rooms had been paid an hourly rate; they were converted to an incentive system.

In-Unit Training Program for Operators
An attempt to train new operators within the production units, using formally designated trainers, was initiated and abandoned as unsuccessful in 1962.

Earnings Development Counseling with Individual Operators
Consulting engineers, working unit by unit, coached low-earning operators on how to improve their performance. Accompanied frequently by the unit supervisor, the engineer would sit with the operator to help her locate her ineffective work methods, encourage her to change to more effective methods, and help her to acquire skill in these methods. Coupled with this was patient encouragement of the operator to increase her skill, her effort, and her effectiveness. An operator was helped in this manner until an outcome was apparent, until her earnings increased, or until she was deemed unlikely to change.

Introduction of Applicant Screening Tests
A program of vision and dexterity testing for selection was inaugurated.

Tightening of Termination Policy for Chronic Absentees
Whereas absence for five consecutive days without excuse had, in theory, previously been grounds for dismissal, this policy had never been enforced. During early 1963 the policy was changed to three consecutive days, and enforcement was begun.

Tightening of Termination Policy for Persistently Low-performing Operators
Late in 1963 an effort was made to locate and terminate those employees whose earnings were chronically low and/or whose absence rates were chronically high.

TABLE 13-1 (Continued)

Vestibule Training Program
A program of vestibule training for new operators, and occasional retraining for experienced operators, was installed in late March 1963.

Training of Managers and Supervisors in Interpersonal Relations
A series of family group sensitivity training laboratories, oriented about interpersonal and role relationships, was held for all members of plant management and supervision.

Blanket 15 Per Cent Adjustment in Rates for Operators in Unit I (The Special-Products Unit)
After the unit system had been created, the unextracted, "speciality" items were left in the original functional operations, which were then consolidated into a production unit labeled Unit I. To restore the rate structure to a level comparable to that existing prior to the extraction of all "long-run" items, it was then necessary to add a 15 per cent bonus to all rates in Unit I. This served to provide extra compensation to operators to make up for losses which they would otherwise sustain in working on only the more difficult styles and materials, under conditions of frequent job variations.

Increase in Minimum Guaranteed Wage by Federal Legislation
September 1, 1963, the Federal Minimum Wage was increased from $1.15 to $1.25.

Group Problem-solving Program with Operators
Designed as a logical extension of the sensitivity training sessions for management, these problem-solving sessions brought together supervisors, their assistants, and operators to (1) post a list of problems which they saw as blocking more effective performance and (2) attempt to solve the problems posted.

Union Recognition and Bargaining
The plant was unionized January 1, 1964.

Early Events—1962

There are two phases of change in productivity to be accounted for in 1962. The first is a fairly steady decline from early January until early August, followed by a rather rapid rise during September and October. This rise stopped short of the level at the beginning of the year.

The first of the new units, Unit III, was put into production during the first week of April. For most operators involved, this change simply meant a physical relocation, as most of them continued doing their regular jobs with the same machine they had been using. Some job changes did occur—for example, the addition of service girls for materials movement—but job standards were adjusted to take account of such changes. Little or no skill relearning was involved. Any improvement in performance for the operator would probably thus be a result of improvement in work space and location, better flow of work, longer runs without job changes, and the like, or of improved morale. Improvements of these kinds ordinarily show their effects rather soon. However, productivity plantwide continued its downward trend, except for a single peak a few weeks before the July vacation. Unit III performed below, not above, the plantwide average for many months. Any productivity gains from this change came much later, and the short-run effect was to depress performance.

Two early events might have had some causal part in the performance rise occurring late in 1962, namely, the first employee attitude survey, and the addition of two professionals to the Weldon staff. The first attitude survey came in the week preceding the lowest point in Weldon's history of operator performance, early August. Within a few weeks came the addition to Weldon's staff of a personnel manager, and another engineer to help the one overburdened man previously on the staff.

Neither of these events was intended or expected to have an immediate effect on operator productivity. Clearly the two new staff members would need some weeks or months, at best, to get oriented to their new situation and to engage in significant activities affecting many operators. The engineer might have had some short-run impact from his own work, as there was at the time an overload of rate complaints, and he handled some of these.

The survey covered a sample of the production employees, but was an event that attracted much notice and discussion. Some people later reported in retrospect that the survey was the first visible activity that indicated to a large number of people that there might be a different approach to personnel matters than what they knew from their past. The survey procedure was itself fairly dramatic, as randomly chosen employees, in groups, on paid time, in the presence of University of Michigan scientists, under conditions of assured anonymity, filled out rather long questionnaires on issues never before openly raised at Weldon.

A fourth change program element came into play later in the year, in November. One of the suggestions which arose out of staff discussions and the survey results was that greater emphasis upon training of new operators might produce beneficial results. Accordingly, in mid-October of that year, nine trainers were appointed from among the ranks of experienced operators, to work with approximately 90 trainees then in the production units. In addition to normal beginning machine instruction, the program provided for standardized follow-up:

1. Checking hourly production rate figures, maintained by each trainee, to locate difficulties
2. Pointing out the trainee's progress to her, and reporting that progress to her supervisor
3. Demonstrating proper sewing methods

The training effort was dispersed over many employees, and the trainers were only part time in this work. There were, in addition, a number of threatening aspects[2] built into the trainer's role.

---

[2] The following quotations from the trainers' instruction sheet illustrate this:

. . . Firmness in enforcing standard method is a must. Resistance to accepting instructions should be reported to the supervisor.
. . . Care should always be exercised not to "spoil" them [the trainees] by doing all the repairs, supplying work, etc.
Daily, the trainer must evaluate whether the employee is satisfactory and when fully decided—recommendation should be made to supervisor if termination should occur.

For these reasons or others, new operator turnover remained as high as ever. In addition, the personnel office became burdened with other tasks and relinquished its involvement to the supervisors. The latter, as they became involved in the then upcoming change to the unit layout system, passed the responsibility to their assistants. By the start of 1963, the program had declined to a marginal level and was terminated as unsuccessful. In any case, this training program could not have had much effect upon operator performance, for it came at the end of a phase of rise in productivity and was followed by an extended period with little or no change in performance.

Can it be said that any of these four elements in the Weldon change program had a positive effect on operator productivity? The activation of Unit III was followed by a decline, and the training program coincided with a leveling-off of a rise in productivity. It would be difficult to argue that they had short-run positive effects. The other two elements, the survey and the staff additions, coincided with a sharp positive change in productivity, and may well have had some impact through their message of hope and good intentions. It seems more plausible, however, to regard the rise in productivity in the late months of 1962 as simply a spontaneous partial recovery from an exceptional midsummer's low level of performance—aided perhaps by the various signs indicating that the new owners did not intend to abandon Weldon nor to disrupt its activities in harsh ways.

Other Minor Program Elements

The preceding section has dealt with four of the sixteen identifiable elements in the Weldon change program—with little evidence to show that they influenced operator performance in the short run. It should be kept in mind that they may have had, and no doubt did have, beneficial effects later on in time or through combination with other later program elements. During 1963 and early 1964 there were introduced several additional elements in the program which clearly had no short-run impact on operator performance; we can dismiss them with a few explanatory words.

Union recognition occurred formally on January 1, 1964, although some employees had no doubt anticipated this result for some weeks or months preceding the event. In any case, the event itself had no immediate positive effect on operator performance, as evidenced by the fact that it came at the end of a period of rising performance and was followed by a leveling-off of this rise.

In September 1963, a new and higher federal minimum wage law became effective. This affected the amount of make-up pay given to low-production employees. In logic, this change might have either raised or depressed performance, for with a higher guarantee, the low operator may see less possibility than before of gaining added earnings through her own skill and effort, while one might equally well argue that those employees receiving higher pay, even though it is unearned, would respond with greater effort to merit the pay. The plantwide productivity curve was unaffected by the change in minimum wage: The event came in the middle of a continuing phase of rising productivity. The effect on individual operators is suggested by the data in Table 13–2, showing that in a sample of 77 operators, ten were at that time earning so little that they could benefit from the new wage law; these ten on the average responded by increasing their productivity by 14 percentage points. It may be added that, of the ten originally below, five went exactly to the new minimum, no higher. The change was not statistically a significant one, and in any case, part of the increase was to be expected in relation to the general, plantwide improvement then in progress.

The formalization of a "tougher" policy for the termination of chronic absentees came in March of 1963, during a period of sharp drop in operator productivity. It affected only a handful of employees at that time and could not have made a noticeable impact on plantwide productivity. However, the actual major change in absenteeism had come earlier—in

TABLE 13-2

EFFECT OF INCREASE IN MINIMUM WAGE,
AUGUST VS. SEPTEMBER, 1963

(mean performance against standard for a random sample of persons earning above and below minimum wage, first week of August vs. first week of September, 1963)

		FIRST WEEK OF AUGUST		FIRST WEEK OF SEPTEMBER			
	NO. OF OPER- ATORS	Mean Per Cent Stand- ard	Stand- ard Devia- tion, %	Mean Per Cent Stand- ard	Stand- ard Devia- tion, %	t	PROBA- BILITY OF CHANCE RESULT
Above new minimum in August	67	121	18	121	21		
Below new minimum in August	10	91	4	105	8	1.35	>.10

October and November of 1962, long before a significant and stabilized rise in operator performance came about. We can dismiss this as a "cause" of improved performance within the scheme of our analysis.

The reorganization of the shipping room, and the introduction of incentive pay for both shipping and cutting room employees, had a marked beneficial effect on the performance of these departments and on the performance of the individual employees. The conversions to incentive pay took place in September 1964 for the shipping department and in March 1963 for the cutting room. It is reasonable to suppose that their improved performance added in some degree to the productivity of operators elsewhere in the plant, but this effect cannot be traced. Their own improvement does not influence our improvement curve figures for the simple reason that they had been excluded from the calculations prior to their "going on standards" and are therefore excluded from subsequent calculations. In any case, their numbers are relatively small in relation to the total plant roster of production employees.

The Main Events

Having disposed of a number of elements in the Weldon program that had no apparent influence in improving operator performance (some apparently having an opposite effect in the short run) we can now turn to the "main" events—those that might have made a big difference. These are:

1. The "unit system"—later phases
2. Vestibule operator training
3. Earnings development counseling
4. Training in interpersonal relations
5. Group problem-solving with operators
6. Blanket rate adjustment in Unit I
7. Employment screening tests
8. Weeding out of low performers

The extension of the unit system beyond the first one, Unit III, was delayed because of the poor results obtained in that first instance. It had been hoped that Unit III would provide an example to the rest of the plant of the feasibility of quick gains in productivity and earnings. This expectation was turned about, as the unit performed less well than the rest of the plant, did not show significant improvement for many months, and lagged behind the rest of the plant even at the end of 1964. Unit IV went into production in January of 1963, and Unit V shortly after, in March. The remaining, high-style garments were then consolidated into Unit I. Unit II (a simple extraction of all sleeve manufacture to a single unit) was started much later, in January of 1964.

Figure 13–3 presents a composite graph showing the effect of conversion to the unit system upon individual operator performance. This figure was made by identifying the individual operators who were later allocated to each of the units, computing the average performance for each of the four sets of operators for the weeks preceding and following the activation of their respective units, and then adjusting the four sets of figures to a common base by setting as zero performance during the fourth week preceding the change. The curve shows that performance declined about five percentage points during the month preceding conversion to the unit system, dropped a further two points immediately after conversion, and then recovered partially, to a new stable level still somewhat below the prechange average.

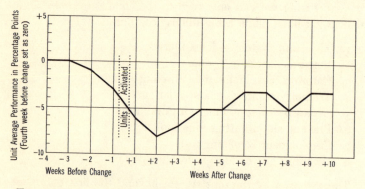

FIGURE 13–3. Weldon: Change in Unit Average Performance in Percentage Points, All Units Combined

It seems apparent, therefore, that the conversion to units did not contribute directly and immediately to improved operator productivity, but instead lowered productivity for at least ten weeks—long enough for the changeover disruptions to have been ironed out. It must be kept in mind, however, that while operator productivity did not show the hoped-for rise, other important gains for the company were no doubt being realized, such as improved quality control, reduced costs other than labor, and stabilized delivery schedules.

Figure 13–4 shows the improvement progress of the four units during 1963 and early 1964. It can be seen that they all

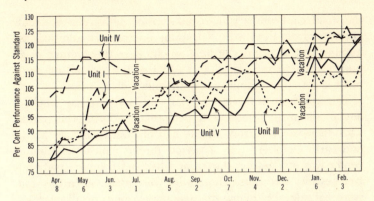

FIGURE 13–4. Weldon: Comparison of Weekly Performance in Sewing Units, April 1963–February 1964

progressed during this time in a similar manner, except that Unit IV was a "quick starter" and Unit III, the first one established, was a laggard to the end.

Vestibule Training

The training center began operations in early April 1963, when operator performance was at a low ebb. Records were kept of the performance of all trainees sent to the sewing units from the time that the center was established until early August 1963. This was a period of sharp recovery in performance. To evaluate the impact of the vestibule training program upon performance during this crucial period, the period was split, and the performance of all employees in the sewing units during the first half was compared to the performance of all employees during the second half. The number of trainees in the units and their performances were also compared for the two periods.

The conclusion from this analysis is that the rise in performance which occurred at this time (roughly from 85 per cent of standard to 100 per cent) cannot be attributed to the better performance of trainees from the vestibule training program. The gain for all employees combined far outweighs the small gain which is noticeable in the performance of new operators from the vestibule training program. In addition, the number of trainees performing much below the average of all operators increased from 6 to 25, so that the over-all improvement is actually diminished by the influx of trainees.

The vestibule training program did not produce much, if any, of the sizable increase in performance during this period. This increase occurred almost entirely between late March and early October 1963, a period during which the training center was just getting started and had fed comparatively few trainees into the units. Those who were assigned to the units were considerably below the average earnings of all operators combined.

In stating that this program does not account for the plant-wide increase in operator productivity, we do not imply that it was without value. On the contrary, as reported in Chapter 8, it no doubt contributed to profitability through other means, e.g., reducing turnover among new operators, reducing cost of training, and permitting the maintenance of an adequate number of operators.

Earnings Development Counseling

A consulting engineer, ordinarily accompanied by the unit supervisor or an assistant supervisor, worked with each operator whose productivity was below a certain cutoff figure until that operator either succeeded in raising her earnings or was abandoned as a lost cause (even though continued on the job). Thus, we expected that this program's effect would have been felt within the time limits of its operation. If effective in raising operator performance, the program should have been associated with an increase in the number of operators who were above the level of performance deemed adequate as a minimum earnings goal.

We compared, for each of the sewing units, the number of earners above the cutoff (set by the engineers as representing "adequate" performance in that unit) at the start of the counseling period with the number of such earners at the end of the period.[3] Success by the earnings counseling engineers is then demonstrated by a significant increase in the number of "adequate" earners during that period of time. We use number rather than percentage because percentage change might simply reflect the termination or transfer of low earners.

Table 13–3 presents the results for each of the four[4] sewing units. These data indicate that earnings development efforts were effective only in units I and III. A possible reason for this immediately presents itself; engineers worked in these two units for a much longer time than in units IV and V. It may be, therefore, that there were more days available per low earner in the former than in the latter. Table 13–3 confirms that this is generally the case: Approximately two engineer-days per low earner were spent in units I and III, whereas only one-half day per low earner was spent in Unit IV and in the first attempt in Unit V. A considerably larger amount of time per low earner was spent in the second attempt in the last-named unit, but the disruption caused by the earlier cessation may well have attenuated any sizable effect. We conclude that the earnings counseling program had a definite beneficial effect where it was intensively applied.

Training Seminars for Supervisors

In evaluating the impact of this training upon operators' earnings, we shall focus our attention upon seminars held in August, September, and October, 1963, for unit supervisors, their assistants, trainers, mechanics, and certain senior clerical employees. The earlier seminars, involving merchandising

---

[3] We used the nonparametric Wilcoxon Composite Rank Test. For each day during the counseling period, we obtained from company records the number of persons in that unit who were earning more than the unit's cutoff score. Similar data were obtained for the same number of days at the end of the earnings development time period. These two groups of days were then rank-ordered in a composite ranking, and a test was conducted to determine the extent to which all of the low ranks occurred at the start and the high ranks at the end of the period.

[4] Unit II had not yet been activated; the employees who later formed it were at this time present in the other four units.

TABLE 13–3

WILCOXON* COMPOSITE RANK TESTS OF NUMBER OF HIGH EARNERS AT START AND END, AND RATIO OF NUMBER OF DAYS TO NUMBER OF LOW EARNERS, IN EARNINGS DEVELOPMENT COUNSELING, BY SEWING UNIT

Unit Experiencing Earnings Development	DURATION IN CALEN- DAR DAYS	RATIO: DAYS TO NUMBER OF LOW EARNERS AT OUTSET	CRITICAL RATIO: RANKED NUMBER OF EARNERS ABOVE EARN- INGS DEVEL- OPMENT CUTOFF AT START AND CLOSE OF PERIOD	PROBABILITY OF CHANCE RESULT
I	135	1.69	2.32	.02
III	113	2.05	2.68	.01
IV	110	0.48	1.08	.28
V (first start, May 1963)	19	0.48	†	> .05
V (second start,‡ Sept. 1963)	38	1.41	0.05	.98

* For all tests the direction of the difference was such that fewer high earners occurred in the early period.

† Because of the small number of cases, the summed ranks had to be interpreted directly from a probability table; that probability is shown.

‡ Engineers had to be extracted from Unit V after three weeks for work in Unit III.

management, top plant management, and a mixture of these two groups, are thought to have been only indirectly relevant to the productivity of operators.

Our method for reviewing the effects of this training upon operator performance was to compare average performance for a period just preceding the August seminar with the performance for the periods following each of the seminars, which came at approximately monthly intervals. There is a weakness in this method, as we assume that the effects, if any, were felt immediately, that there were no delayed effects, and that none of the other change program elements were particularly active at the time. Nevertheless, these seminars coincide with the sharpest phase of increasing operator productivity, and it seems possible to attribute this rise, in part, to the supervisory training seminars.

For the plant as a whole, although increases were occurring prior to training, the greater (i.e., statistically more significant) further increases in operator productivity do come, as expected, the further the series of sessions progresses. This is shown in the probability column for total plant in Table 13-4.

We should expect similar results for each of the four units separately (Unit II had not yet been activated). Table 13-4 shows that for units III and IV, the results are more or less as expected, with the significance of the operators' improvement corresponding roughly to the proportion of supervisors trained. In units I and V, however, the improvement in operator performance is most significant after the August seminar when only a few supervisors had attended (Unit I) or none at all (Unit V); in Unit I the later seminars were not followed by further operator improvement, while in Unit V there is the expected significant improvement after the September seminar, attended by a majority of supervisors from that unit. We can say, then, that the training was effective in the case of units III and IV, partially effective in Unit V, and not effective in Unit I.

This conclusion, if valid, should be supported by the figures for each of the subunits composing the whole units. There are nine such subunits having identifiable assistant supervisors and sufficient data to analyze. These results are summarized in Table 13-5.

Unit I trousers subunit shows an operator improvement after the August session—which neither the assistant nor the supervisor attended. The pressing unit shows no significant operator

TABLE 13-4

Wilcoxon Composite Ranks Tests of Effect on Operators' Performance of Sensitivity Seminars for Supervisors and Assistants, for Units and Total Plant

Comparison Periods (each period about 3 weeks)	CRITICAL RATIOS: SUMMED RANKS FOR EACH COMPARISON PERIOD										PERCENTAGE ATTENDANCE				
	Unit I		Unit III		Unit IV		Unit V		Total Plant		Unit I	Unit III	Unit IV	Unit V	Total Plant
	z	Probability of Chance Result	z	Probability of Chance Result	z	Probability of Chance Result	z	Probability of Chance Result	z	Probability of Chance Result					
2nd mo. prior to training vs. 1 mo. prior to training (control period)	3.84	<.001	7.02	<.001	1.95*	.05	3.05*	<.01	5.45	<.001					
Pre-August session vs. post-August	4.62	<.001	1.94	.05	4.41*	<.001	7.24	<.001	3.29	<.001	14%	40%	11%	0%	15%
Pre-Sept. session vs. post-Sept. session	1.64	.10	2.62	.01	4.83	<.001	2.15	.03	3.62	<.001	38%	40%	44%	67%	38%
Pre-Oct. session vs. post-Oct. session	0.64	.54	3.32	<.001	1.94	.05	0.57	.57	7.62	<.001	19%	20%	22%	33%	31%

TABLE 13–5

WILCOXON TESTS OF EFFECT ON OPERATORS' PERFORMANCE OF
ASSISTANT SUPERVISOR'S ATTENDANCE AT SENSITIVITY SEMINARS,
BY SUBUNIT

| Subunit | CRITICAL RATIO | | | EFFECT SHOULD FOLLOW |
	August Seminar	September Seminar	October Seminar	
I—trousers	−3.76*	−1.47	−1.60	September
I—pressing	−1.02	−1.81	−1.04	September
III—coats	−0.38‡	−3.94†	−2.19*	September
III—trousers	−4.57*	−0.53‡	−1.30	August
III—pressing	−4.97†	−0.94‡	−2.81†	October
IV—trousers	−4.30†‡	−4.36†	−1.08	September
V—coats (supv.)	−7.46†	−1.04	−0.02‡	September
V—trousers }same	−1.40‡	−1.15	−0.60	October
V—pressing }asst.	−6.30†	−1.68	−0.74	October

* Probability less than .05.
† Probability less than .01.
‡ Preperiod earnings *better* than postperiod.

improvement between successive time segments. The improvement for Unit I as a whole, therefore, must arise from improvements in the coat subunit following the August seminar which
two of the four assistants attended (not shown in Table 13–5).
Units III and IV appear as predicted, with subunit operator
performance gains coming at times compatible with the seminar attendance of the supervisors and assistants.

The subunit analysis for Unit V shows the performance gain
following the August session came from at least two of the
subunits—but no one from these units attended the August
seminar. A smaller but significant improvement in the coats
subunit following the September session corresponds with the
attendance at that session of the supervisor and one other
person, the operator trainer. There was but one assistant supervisor in Unit V; she attended the October session, but no
significant performance improvement followed. Any effect on

performance in Unit V therefore must be attributed to the training of the supervisor himself.

In summary: The subunit analysis offers some additional support to the earlier conclusions. It appears that the interpersonal relations training "took" quite well in units III and IV, in the sense that operator improvement corresponds fairly well with the schedule of training session attendance. For Unit I, the only effect was upon a pair of assistant supervisors in one subunit. For Unit V, the modest effect appears to be associated only with the training of the supervisor.

Can any other events reasonably have caused the substantial increases in operator productivity that occurred at this time? In the case of Unit IV, no other element in the change program seems relevant, for the layout changes in this unit had been made months before and the earnings development work had ended months before; seasonal changeover had not just occurred. In the case of Unit III, the operator earnings development activity overlapped the interpersonal relations training; however, an analysis of the impact of earnings development shows that the gain from this work in Unit III came early, prior to the first interpersonal relations training session, and already had diminished as an element in operator productivity improvement. We conclude, therefore, that the substantial productivity gains during the August–October period appear to be associated primarily with the training of supervisors and staff. The evidence, however, is tenuous.

Group Problem-solving with Operators

Following the training of supervisors and other staff in interpersonal relations, August–October 1963, the Weldon change program moved into a related area to carry group participative processes and problem resolution down to the level of the operators. This program is described in Chapter 10.

Our analysis of the impact of this program is limited wholly to Units III and IV. In Unit III initial sessions were held early in October 1963, with follow-up sessions later in the same month. In Unit IV, similar sessions took place in January and February 1964.[5]

The evaluation of the effect of this program on operator performance in Units III and IV rests upon the comparison of productivity for periods preceding and following the problem-solving sessions, and using Units I and V for the same periods as a comparison and control.

In the case of Unit III, the results uncovered a surprising fact: This unit showed no significant difference in performance between "before" and "after" periods, while the two control units improved significantly. A background event explains this anomaly. Unit III, much more than the other units, is adversely affected by seasonal product changes, and the seasonal change came just as the problem-solving sessions were completed. Any possible short-run gain from problem-solving meetings is completely masked by the seasonal upset. In this connection, however, it is useful to compare the productivity of Unit III during this seasonal change with its performance the previous year. In 1963, the seasonal downturn associated with style change began during the fourth week of October and bottomed at the end of November; full recovery was achieved in mid-January—a total time span of ten weeks. In the prior year, 1962, the recovery took thirteen weeks, even though the drop was only half as deep (but from a level of productivity already quite low). Thus, it may be argued that after problem-solving sessions, Unit III was able to recover from a drastic drop (15 percentage points) more quickly than otherwise would have been the case.

When similar problem-solving sessions were held several

---

[5] In the case of Unit I, an initial session was held much later, in September 1964, and there were no follow-up sessions because a severe inventory imbalance disrupted production, and the supervisor and her assistants felt they had interpersonal conflicts to be resolved before further operator involvement. In Unit V, initial sessions were held in March 1965, with follow-up on an informal basis rather than in group meetings. In Unit II, the problem-solving activity also came after the period of this report. These activities came after the 1963 rise in operator productivity and are ignored in this analysis.

months later for Unit IV, the data indicated that all three compared units—Unit IV and the two control units, I and V—showed a statistically significant improvement in operator productivity, but that the change for Unit IV was less likely to have been a result of chance. Whereas the change for the control units was an improvement of 4 per cent of standard, Unit IV improved by 8 per cent. These findings suggest that benefit was derived in Unit IV from the group problem-solving work.

Rate Adjustment in Unit I

Unit I operators, after the formation of Units III, IV and V, were left with a work mix that was almost entirely "high style," requiring slower work pace, more frequent job changes, more complex tasks. While the rates for individual jobs were fair for a "normal" mix of products, they were judged to be too tight under the changed conditions. Management elected voluntarily to provide a blanket rate adjustment of 15 per cent to all operator rates in Unit I. This step in the change program was taken for simple reasons of equity, but was thought to have potential effects beyond the 15 per cent and outside of the unit directly affected.

Anecdotal accounts by the consulting engineers and others suggest that the goodwill created by this prompt and voluntary rate adjustment extended beyond Unit I. There is, however, no evidence in the operator production figures to sustain this view. Unit I operators rose almost instantly beyond the 15 per cent expected by the adjustment, but soon settled back to almost exactly 15 per cent; there was no improvement in performance attributable to the rate adjustment. During the same period, Unit IV showed a leveling off (after a period of increase which occurred prior to Unit I's rate adjustment), Unit III showed little or no change, and Unit V showed a moderate increase probably arising from earnings counseling work then in progress.

We conclude that the 15 per cent rate adjustment in Unit I

had no effect on operator productivity, although it altered the index for that unit itself.

Selection Tests

Selection tests were first used in March 1963, shortly before vestibule training was begun. These two programs were, in fact, coordinated recommendations of the same consulting group. Since all newly hired operators entered employment through the training center, and because the impact of vestibule training was not great enough during 1963 to figure as a "cause" of the major performance increase during that year, we may dismiss selection tests also as a "cause."

Still, it is worth noting that three tests were used; a test of finger dexterity, a test of manual dexterity, and a test of visual acuity. Although the actual impact of using these tests upon the sizable performance improvement which was then occurring was negligible, their potential (and probably actual) contribution to good performance may be quite great in the long run. Weldon's records on trainees show that even among those who passed the tests and were employed, those scoring relatively high were less likely to quit before completion of training and were quicker to get to standard performance levels.

Termination of Chronic Low Performers and Chronic Absentees

Between late November 1963 and January 1964, an effort was made to get rid of the remaining employees with chronically low production records and histories of frequent absence. The old firm's emphasis on total dozens of garments produced, regardless of cost, had led to the prolonged retention and repeated rehiring of many ineffective employees who showed no signs of responding as others had to the efforts to improve their performance. It was decided to terminate these people at an early date.

Figures for the period (Figure 13–5) show a decline in total numbers of sewing unit operators, with a rather sharp decline from December 1963 onward into early January. Average operator performance at this time was rising—about eight percentage points.

Our immediate question is whether the increase in average productivity, November through January, is due to these terminations. We find that the average productivity of those employees not terminated rose by 3 percentage points during this period.[6] The remaining 5 percentage points of increase might therefore be due to the termination policy, unless there were other change events also active at the time. In fact, the period included no other plausible "causes" for the increase in average productivity. Union recognition is not thought to have had a noticeable effect, since it was expected; Unit II was activated, but this would normally depress rather than raise productivity in the short run; the earnings development counseling was then in progress in Unit V, but, as noted before, without measurable influence on productivity. We therefore conclude that a rise of about 5 percentage points in average productivity was brought about by the termination of low performers.

An Overview: Factors Influencing Operator Performance

This chapter has been an attempt to isolate the specific elements of the Weldon change program that might be shown

---

[6] The impact can be calculated in the following manner: Weigh the mean percentage of standard on December 3 by the total number of sewing unit employees on that date; from this subtract the number of low earners no longer present on January 27, multiplied by an estimate of their mean percentage of standard, and then divide by the number of employees on January 27. Assuming that the numbers in the other categories of performance do not change appreciably (they do not), the resulting new mean percentage of standard should miss the actual mean percentage for January 27 only by the extent of improvement in the performance of those who remain. When we calculate this, we find that our predicted percentage of standard is 112, whereas the actual new percentage is 115. The number of low earners was weighted by 84 per cent of standard, which was the personnel manager's estimate of their actual performance at that time.

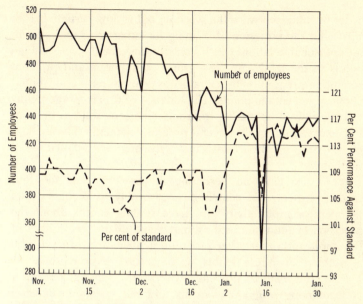

FIGURE 13–5. Weldon: Total Number and Performance Against Standard of Sewing Unit Employees by Day, November 1, 1963– January 30, 1964

to have influenced the large rise in average operator productivity. The rise—from about 85 per cent of standard to over 115 per cent of standard—occurred largely between April 1963 and January 1964, although some came later. Our attention has been focused on this span of less than one year.

Because of their nature and the time of their occurrence, a number of change program elements were eliminated from further consideration; they could not, or it is evident that they did not, affect productivity in the short run. Eight change elements have been given more intensive examination. Four of these were shown to have no discernible impact on performance by the methods available for our analysis.

Our final estimate from this analytic procedure is that the earnings development program with individual operators was the most potent of the steps undertaken, contributing perhaps 11 percentage points of the total gain of 30 points. Next in order of influence were the weeding out of low earners in late 1963, and the provision of training for supervisors and staff in interpersonal relations, each contributing about 5 percentage points to the total gain. The group consultation and problem resolution program with operators appears to have contributed about 3 percentage points. The balance of 6 percentage points can be viewed as arising from miscellaneous sources or from the combination of the several program elements. The method of arriving at these statistical estimates is detailed in a footnote.[7]

While we have no hesitation in asserting that the four named elements did contribute measurably to Weldon's gain in operator productivity, we have serious doubts about the precision of the numerical estimates and about the validity of the implication that other program elements contributed little or nothing. For these doubts, we have three basic reasons.

First, the analysis procedure necessarily ignored the interaction among program elements and the systemic character of the total program. The changes were not introduced in any neatly experimental way designed to allow separate evaluation of each element. On the contrary, the theory guiding the program holds that the elements are all mutually interdependent, and, in principle, not separable (even though some

---

[7] The steps in calculating how much of the total improvement in operator performance can be statistically attributed to each of the program elements were as follows:

1. The change during the period April 1, 1963, to January 30, 1964, is treated as occurring in three installments: April 1 to May 13, July 8 to September 23, and December 30 to January 23.

2. The improvement in performance against standard for each unit is multiplied by the number of employees in the unit on the terminal day, and these products are then added across all units.

3. Each product is then divided by the sum of products to calculate a percentage of over-all net change attributable to the unit.

4. This percentage of net change is then multiplied for each unit by the global change figure during that subperiod for all sewing units combined. This provides the percentage of standard improvement attributable to the performance improvement of that unit.

5. This percentage is then ascribed to, or divided among, the events during that period, as they appeared in the earlier analysis.

6. Percentages are accumulated by change event or change program.

relatively more potent factors might be distinguished). The theory holds, furthermore, that an "open" organizational system will be affected not only by events in its environment (e.g., model changes) but by phases of change arising from unplanned coincidence of the effects of short-term and longer-term changes. For example, we might well speculate that the large immediate impact of the earnings development counseling—demonstrated in our data—could not have occurred unless preceded by the conversion to the unit system of production with rationalization of jobs, correction of rates, and improved production planning. The latter change element cannot be shown to have "its own" impact on operator performance; yet it is more than merely plausible to suggest that counseling of operators would be futile if the work environment had been left in irrational confusion. The effective and successful weeding out of remaining low performers later in the program was no doubt made possible by the prior events that had increased earnings for most operators and had provided reassurance of the humanitarian values of the managers. Other similar interactive relations among program elements no doubt also occurred.

Second, although the "technical" changes at Weldon were on a large scale and affected nearly every employee, we find from our analysis that these changes cannot be shown to have improved operator performance. One reason, of course, is that job reorganization does not necessarily require better job performance, but may only permit it to happen. Another reason is that most of the technical changes were accompanied by new job specifications and rates such that large increases in physical output arising from simplification or mechanization of work did not necessarily alter performance for individuals relative to standard. A large improvement in the functioning of the production system as a whole can occur without individual improvement in standard performance. Studies in other firms have shown that large gains in over-all unit cost performance may well come about even while individual job performance is declining. Our analytic method was unfair to the engineers, whose work at Weldon is better evaluated in terms of total system performance than in terms of individual operator performance.

A third consideration is that the very notion of specific external "causes" of behavior change in operators is at odds with our knowledge of human behavior. The "real" causes of Weldon's improvement in operator performance lie within the operators themselves, for it is their human accommodation to changing circumstance that we are assessing, more than the circumstances themselves. Weldon operators, like most other people, prefer—given a fair chance—to work effectively, to earn more, to do a good job, to aid the system of which they are a part.

For all these valid disclaimers, we still think it significant that the most immediately potent factors in performance improvement are, for the most part, those aimed at altering the relationships among people and their relationships to their work situation.

14

EMPLOYEE ATTITUDES, MOTIVATIONS, AND SATISFACTIONS

———

David G. Bowers and Stanley E. Seashore

THE EFFECTIVENESS OF an organization can be assessed with confidence only if many aspects of performance are taken into account. The preceding chapters report Weldon's improvement in organizational output, conservation of resources, and individual work performance. These are important indicators, but not the only ones. We turn now to another category of criteria by which Weldon may be judged: Do the Weldon people view their organization with greater confidence and optimism? Do they get more personal satisfaction from their work situation? Are their personal motives more closely linked to Weldon's organizational requirements?

We take the view that it is desirable, in itself, that these queries be answered positively. It is reasonable for an organization to aim to increase, within some limits, its "output" of satisfaction, motivation, and positive feelings. For some organizations, indeed, these are the main goals. Also, there is some reason for believing, as many managers do, that the performance and survival of an industrial organization over a span of years may well be contingent upon its provision of satisfaction, motivation, and positive affect.

With this in mind, we made an attempt to measure Weldon's performance in these areas before, during, and after the improvement program, and to get comparable measures from the main Harwood plant. The method used was the anonymous questionnaire completed by random samples of nonsupervisory employees in the two plants.[1] This chapter will summarize the survey results with respect to:

1. Respondent's personal background and job values
2. Attitudes about the company, his own job, work effort, compensation, and fellow employees
3. Expectations about the future
4. Perceptions of change

Personal Background

Average educational achievement, the proportion of women, and the proportion of married employees were similar in the two plants in 1962. Responses to these questions changed little, and remained similar in 1964. In each plant, about 90 per cent of the employees were women, about three-quarters were married, and the average education was "some high school" (see Table 14–1).

The two plants differed in average employee age and in length of service. Before the Weldon improvement program, about a third of the employees were under 25 years of age and a third were of less than two years' service, while for Harwood, the figures were near zero. By the fall of 1964, Weldon had diminished substantially its proportions of young

---

[1] The questionnaire, slightly extended in content between the 1962 and the 1964 surveys, was administered to respondents in groups, on paid time, by a representative of the University of Michigan. Respondents were chosen randomly from the payroll rosters, excluding employees of very short service. Participation was voluntary, although urged, and the refusal rate was negligible. The numbers in the various samples ranged from 144 (Weldon, 1963) to 46 (Harwood, 1964.) The questionnaires were administered in late summer 1962, and in midfall 1964, with a supplemental survey at Weldon in August 1963.

TABLE 14–1

COMPARISONS AND CHANGES IN PERSONAL BACKGROUND OF HARWOOD AND WELDON EMPLOYEES, 1962, 1963, AND 1964

Personal Background	WELDON 1962	t*	HARWOOD 1962	t*	WELDON 1963	t*	WELDON 1964	t*	HARWOOD 1964
25 years old or under	0%	Sig.	36%		34%	Sig.	13%		0%
Female	85		92		88		92		91
High school graduate and above	38		43		43		35		30
Married	74		65		58		70		83
Less than 2 years' service	2	Sig.	35		42	Sig.	16	Sig.	0

NOTE: The figures show the percentages of respondents checking the most favorable (or in some cases, most unfavorable) of the response categories offered in the multiple-choice questionnaire. Each item indicates whether the response categories are on the favorable or unfavorable end of the scale. There were 143 Weldon respondents in 1962, 144 in 1963, and 111 in 1964. Harwood had 47 respondents in 1962 and 46 in 1964.

* The *t* test for the significance of the difference between means at the .05 level was used to compare percentages in adjacent columns in each row.

and short-service employees, and was approaching the Harwood condition. These facts derive from the initial difference in policy of the two plants, one emphasizing the building of an experienced, stable work force, and the other relying on temporary seasonal additions to handle the work load. The data from the surveys simply reflect the change in Weldon's policy and the subsequent efforts to reduce turnover and to eliminate the ineffective, unstable (and generally younger) employees. Those remaining were, of course, older on average and had longer service, as the survey results show.

The two plants were remarkably alike in 1962 in what their

employees said they wanted from a job. They remained alike in 1964, although some minor changes did occur. Figure 14–1 shows the survey results. The one change to be noted in the

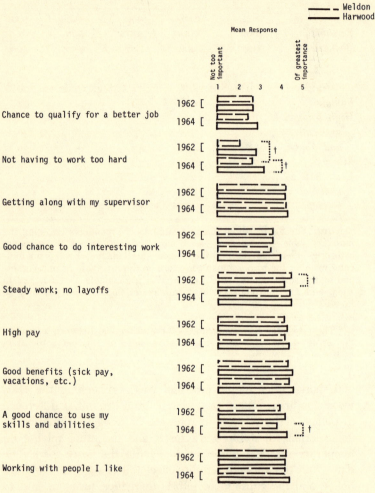

FIGURE 14–1. Importance of Nine Job Characteristics*

* These nine job characteristics appear as nine separate questions on the questionnaire. Number of respondents: Weldon 1962 = 144, 1964 = 111; Harwood 1962 = 47, 1964 = 46.

† Significant difference at .05 level.

views of Weldon employees concerns "not having to work too hard." In 1962 the Weldon people attached much less importance to this than did Harwood employees. This seems to reflect the simple and uncomplicated fact that Weldon employees were not working as hard then as Harwood employees. By 1964, when the productivity levels of both plants were indistinguishable, their rating of this job factor was approaching Harwood's level, although in both plants this remained one of the least important factors in judging a job. In general, one can say that the Weldon improvement program had very little impact at all, and certainly no adverse impact, on the employees' views of what they wanted from their jobs.

Opinions About the Company

The Weldon improvement program, also, had rather little effect upon the attitudes of employees toward their company, although attitudes did improve from a neutral to a more positive position. By 1964 the employees considered the Weldon company to be more concerned than in 1962 about the welfare of employees, more ready to make innovations, and more ready to give information about the future. In the main, however, attitudes regarding the company itself were slow to respond to objectively large improvements in the conditions experienced by the employees.

In 1962, Harwood employees were definitely more favorable than the Weldon people in their attitudes toward their respective companies. By 1964, this difference had actually increased on most issues, because the improvement at Harwood exceeded that of Weldon.[2]

The figures for the seven questionnaire items are shown in the first block of Table 14–2, and a global index of attitude toward company is shown in Figure 14–2.

---

[2] The greater improvement in attitude toward the company at the comparison plant is a matter of some curiosity. Although opinions are available as to the reasons for this change they are highly speculative. Exploring them would be beyond the scope of the present report.

TABLE 14–2

Comparisons and Changes in Questionnaire Responses, 1962, 1963, and 1964

	WELDON 1962	t†	HARWOOD 1962	t†	WELDON 1963	t†	WELDON 1964	t†	HARWOOD 1964
The Company									
*Better or much better than most	40%	Sig.	22%		26%	Sig.	28%	Sig.	56%
*Fairly or very quick to use improved methods	53	Sig.	18	Sig.	30	Sig.	24	Sig.	59
Somewhat or very interested in welfare and happiness of employees	44	Sig.	26		38	Sig.	41	Sig.	74
*Often try and really try to improve working conditions	60	Sig.	32		34		33	Sig.	71
*Usually or almost always give information regarding future	25		30	Sig.	40	Sig.	40		44
*Good or very good job planning, private problems	42	Sig.	22		30		26	Sig.	65
*Fairly or very easy to get fair hearing from top management	56		42		46		43	Sig.	61
The Job									
Having no temporary job changes within last month	83	Sig.	65		63	Sig.	78		89

*Strongly prefer no permanent change to another job	83	Sig.	76	71	Sig.	79		89
*Strongly prefer no temporary change to another job	77		60	65	Sig.	74		70
*Job gives very or fairly good chance to do best	54		71	60		78		76
*Find work somewhat or very satisfying and interesting	89		77	80		84		87
Often or very often delayed by poor service	20		24	23		21		15
Rates generally set so all or most can make out	59	Sig.	48	51		56	Sig.	76
Rates own job somewhat or much tighter than for others	42		26	35		36		41
Rates will become somewhat or much tighter	32		35	34		29		28
Effort								
*Usually produce much or somewhat more than the rate calls for	60	Sig.	44	50	Sig.	67	Sig.	89
*Work very or extremely hard	66	Sig.	47	53	Sig.	67	Sig.	48
Expect long-run production to be much or somewhat higher than now	40	Sig.	63	60	Sig.	55	Sig.	32

COMPARISONS AND CHANGES IN QUESTIONNAIRE RESPONSES, 1962, 1963, AND 1964 (*continued*)

	WELDON 1962	t†	HARWOOD 1962	t†	WELDON 1963	t†	WELDON 1964	t†	HARWOOD 1964
Compensation									
*Very or quite satisfied with pay	40	Sig.	22	Sig.†	19		27	Sig.	39
*Pay somewhat or much lower than comparable jobs in community	8	Sig.	38		36	Sig.	28	Sig.	15
*Differences in earnings to no or very little extent reflect differences in ability and effort (vs. luck and opportunity)	40		24		28		18	Sig.	35
*Company makes quite or great deal of effort to help new employees maintain income	51	Sig.	26	Sig.	44	Sig.	44	Sig.	63
Fellow Employees									
Say employees would moderately or strongly disapprove of a person who consistently turns out the most work	30	Sig.	42		41		42	Sig.	28

Item	1962		1963		1964		1962		1964
*No or little unreasonable pressure from peers for better performance	83		82		81		86		93
*Like fellow employees quite a bit or a great deal	89	Sig.	85		84	Sig.	86	Sig.	100
*Depend upon other employees quite a lot or a great deal for suggestions and advice	24		20		17		11	Sig.	28
*To considerable or very great extent feels he and other employees belong to team that work together	66	Sig.	45		53		59	Sig.	71
*Say employees in his department are above average or one of best groups, at sticking together or helping each other	30		25		30		25		24

NOTE: The figures show the percentages of respondents checking the two most favorable (or, in some cases, most unfavorable) of the response categories offered in the multiple-choice questionnaire. Each item indicates whether the response categories are on the favorable or unfavorable end of the scale. The number of Weldon respondents in 1962 was 143, 144 in 1963, and 111 in 1964. Harwood had 47 respondents in 1962 and 46 in 1964.

* Items are charted in Figure 14–2.
† The t test for the significance of the difference between means at the .05 level was used.
‡ Over-all difference is significant in a negative direction.

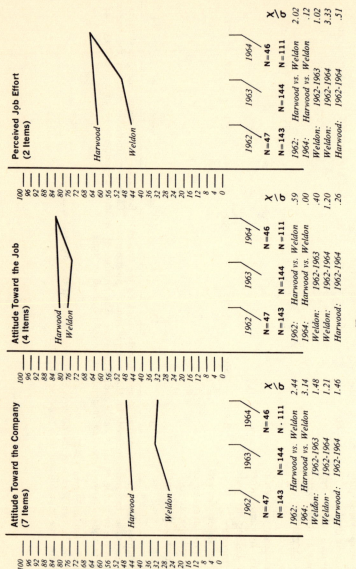

FIGURE 14-2.

N = number of respondents.

NOTE: Items composing these indexes appear in Table 14-2 and have been marked (*) for easy identification. Shown are the mean percentages of respondents checking the two most favorable (or, in some cases, most unfavorable) of the response categories offered in the multiple-choice questionnaire.

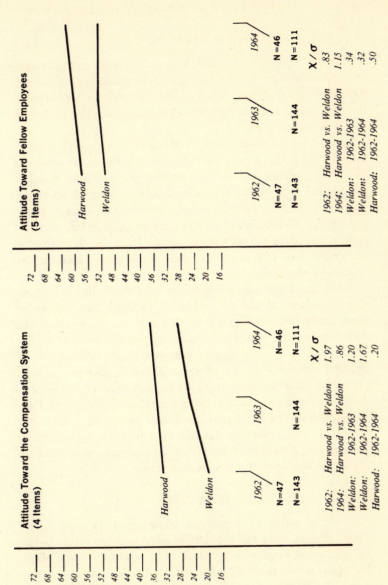

FIGURE 14–2 (continued)

Opinions About Own Job

A global index of job attitudes, also in Figure 14–2, shows that employees of both plants were generally quite positive about their jobs and that there were neither any differences between the two plants nor any significant changes over the period of the Weldon program.

Table 14–2 (second block) elaborates this general impression. In 1962, the significant differences between respondents of the two plants had to do with the changes from one job assignment to another. The unnecessary shifting of operators was recognized by most consultant observers as a major problem of the Weldon plant at the time of acquisition, and the survey responses reflect that situation. By 1964, the situation at Weldon had improved, and the survey results confirm the reports of observers.

Table 14–2 also reports opinions relating to the incentive-rate structures of the two plants. Questions were asked in three areas: the rates generally, the rate on the respondent's own regular job, and what would happen to rates within the next year. No meaningful between-plant differences or changes occurred on any of these items. Employees in both plants felt that the rates were set so that most of the experienced operators could attain reasonable earnings, if they worked hard. They also perceived their own rates to be about the same as the rates on the jobs held by other operators, or perhaps just a bit tighter, and they felt that rates would remain about the same for the foreseeable future.

Work Effort

The global index of perceived work effort (Figure 14–2) shows that in 1962 the Weldon employees were much below the Harwood employees in their own report of work effort. By 1964, when their actual productivity had risen substantially, the Weldon people reported themselves to be working harder and at Harwood's level. The actual change is matched by the attitude change.

The details of this change (Table 14–2, section on work

effort) are of some interest. At the end of the Weldon improvement program, the employees, in increasing proportion, felt they were producing as much or more than the rates called for, and that they worked very hard or extremely hard; a decreasing proportion felt that there would be future rises in productivity. At the same time, the views of the Harwood people, while remaining constant on the average, actually changed in two opposite ways: In 1964 more felt their production to be above that called for by the rates, while fewer felt they were working very or extremely hard. In both plants, a diminishing proportion of employees expected further increases in productivity in the future.

Compensation

During the period of the Weldon improvement program, the attitude of employees toward their compensation system became more favorable. During the same period, the Harwood employees, initially much more favorable in attitude, also improved their position. The improvement at Weldon was the greater, as might be expected in view of the actual increase in employee earnings during the period (Figure 14–2).

The Weldon improvement appears in all four of the questionnaire items relating to compensation, but is particularly strong with respect to Weldon's effort to help new employees to achieve a high income. These changes are shown in Table 14–2 (section on compensation). The changes for Harwood, while generally consistent and favorable, were not significant. During 1963, there was a small decline in the proportion of Weldon employees who expressed satisfaction with their pay; this might be attributed to the fact that at that time their pay was still low, and the management was, in effect, urging that they consider their earnings to be unreasonably low.

Fellow Employees

Weldon employees in 1962 held generally positive attitudes toward their fellow employees; by 1964 there was a slight but nonsignificant improvement in their attitudes. Initially, the

Harwood employees were more favorable than the Weldon employees in their attitudes, and the slight change at Harwood by 1964 is also insignificant. These data are represented in Figure 14–2; Table 14–2 provides supporting details.

The Future

Employees at both plants were asked about the changes they expected in the future, and about their own personal plans for staying or leaving. On the first question, there were no meaningful differences between the two plants nor any significant change during the period of the Weldon improvement program; at both plants the prevailing and constant view was that "things will stay about the same as they are now."

On the second question, there was a substantial change in the case of Weldon. Initially, in 1962, about half of the Weldon employees said they were definitely planning to leave or that they would leave under certain conditions of opportunity or convenience. This is an extremely high rate of declared potential defection from a company. By 1964, a very substantial majority were planning to stay on indefinitely. The change reflects both the removal of some transient employees and also the making of Weldon into a more attractive place of employment.

Perceptions of Change

One of the concerns of the Weldon management during the improvement program was that the changes affecting employees might be excessively frequent and disturbing. Steps were taken of several kinds to stabilize work situations and to confine changes to those most likely to improve results. The surveys at Weldon included special questions to assess the employees' experience of changes and their view of whether the changes improved their work situations. The questions referred to six different specific changes, listed in Table 14–3, and were asked with reference to the year preceding each survey.

TABLE 14-3

PERCEPTIONS OF IMPACT OF CHANGES BY WELDON RESPONDENTS

Nature of Change	YEAR	PERCEIVED IMPACT			
		No Change	Change, But No Effect	Better Off	Worse Off
Supervisor changed	1963	63%	18%	12%	7%
(different	1964	51	27	11	11
supervisor)					
Change in	1963	75	4	10	11
regular job	1964	77	5	10	8
assignment					
Change in	1963	33	15	10	10
machinery or	1964	79	4	8	5
equipment					
Changed	1963	9	28	21	10
workplace	1964	57	24	14	4
Change in kinds	1963	44	11	8	9
of garments	1964	53	12	9	24
worked on					
Breakup of	1963	27	24	15	8
work group	1964	60	24	8	6

The striking result, evident in the table, is that in both years—periods of very extensive changes—only a minority of employees recalled having personally experienced each of the possible changes. Furthermore, about half of those having any given change said that it made no significant difference for them, the remainder splitting about equally in saying the change was for the better or for the worse. It is factual that some few employees experienced none of the six kinds of change, and that some others were exposed to several of them. On the whole, we believe that the employees had "forgotten" some of the changes they experienced even quite recently, and that they adapted so quickly to the changes that they understated the impact, whether for better or for worse. There was no widespread feeling of general disruption of work arrangements, no widespread feeling of great benefit from the changes. These results are in marked contrast to those found in some other organizations, in which relatively minor changes (by objective standards) have been thought very threatening and disruptive by the employees affected.

Discussion

It is commonly believed by managers that employee attitudes, motivations, and satisfactions are likely to fluctuate in response to immediate events—that they are essentially unstable and easily changed. Our survey results at Weldon do not support this view. The general picture that emerges is one of stability and moderate change. Rather dramatic changes in policy, in work arrangements, in interpersonal relationships—and in work performance and pay—were in Weldon accompanied by only modest affective and motivational changes. It is as though the Weldon employees had been ready to adapt their work behavior to the new situation but were cautious and reserved in changing their views and judgments.

Such change as did occur was favorable to the firm's program goals. At the end of the change program period there was a more positive view of the company, an awareness of the reduction in disruptive temporary job changes, more satisfaction with the compensation system and with pay, more willingness to plan for continued employment with Weldon. The increase in feelings of having to work hard was accompanied by an increase, not a decrease, in satisfactions and positive attitudes.

At the end of 1964, the Weldon employees' view of their company and their work situation, while improved, remained less favorable than that of Harwood employees, and less favorable than that of employees in various other firms we have studied in similar ways. Improvements of equal magnitude occurred during the same period in the Harwood plant, where there is a much longer history of efforts toward introducing conditions that merit favorable employee attitudes and satisfactions.

From these results and observations, we suggest that basic gains in the "output" of an organization with respect to satisfactions, motivations, and positive feelings often may be harder to achieve than gains in cost performance and work output. Such gains may well take place over a long span of time; employees may reserve judgment about the personal meaning of the policy and work system changes until the passage of time has allowed proof of their validity and proof of the stability of the new conditions of life. Distrust of management, habits of noncooperation and disinterest, suspicions about the motives of others, and bargaining about work effort are learned early by many people in their experiences at work; these are not easily altered during a brief two-year effort toward achieving a more trustful, open, cooperative, and self-determining organizational system.

15

THE NEW ORGANIZATIONAL SYSTEM

David G. Bowers

IN REVIEWING the results of the Weldon program, we have so far taken up three aspects of performance: the productivity and economy of the organization as a whole, the productivity of individual operators, and the personal reactions of the operators to changing conditions at the Weldon plant. We now turn to a fourth and final part of this report of results. In this chapter, we review the results of Weldon's effort to introduce a new organizational system.

By an "organizational system," we refer, first, to a "philosophy" of management—a set of guiding assumptions, values, and principles that are intended to form the basis for managerial behavior and activities within the organization. Secondly, we refer to the patterns of activities, and role relationships, derived from the philosophy, that bear upon the decisions made by the organization and upon the communicating, coordinating, controlling, and related functions at all levels and in all parts of the organization. This chapter accordingly will be concerned with: leadership, control, supervision, motivation, communication, interaction, decision-making, and goal-setting.

The method is similar to that represented in earlier chapters. Attempts to measure Weldon's condition before, during, and after the change program will be reported, and Weldon will be compared with Harwood. The account will be divided into three parts, according to the measurement instruments and concepts used. The first part will deal with supervisory leadership and the second with the amount and distribution of control within the organization; the third part will give a global assessment of change in the nature of Weldon's management system.

Supervisory Leadership

Early in the study, several problems concerned with lower-level leadership and supervision were obvious to the consultants and observers who visited the Weldon plant. Three stood out above all others:

There were too many employees per supervisor. This is not a judgment from an arbitrary view about the appropriate span of control; instead, it is a judgment arising from the observation that many people in formal positions of "supervision" at Weldon were not in fact functioning as supervisors in the accepted meaning of the term. In the production areas, only the five sewing room supervisors (unit heads) engaged in truly supervisory activities, and even they were almost devoid of authority. The ratio of supervisors and managers possessing some significant authority to the number of production employees was about one to each 150 employees—a very large ratio compared to that prevailing in industry. By comparison, at the Harwood plant, even the assistant supervisors had more authority than the Weldon head supervisors, and the ratio was estimated to be about one supervisor to 30 production employees. Under such conditions, no matter how energetic and well-intentioned a Weldon supervisor was, it was not physically possible for him to work in any effective way with the people under his direction.

The Weldon supervisors were skilled in the methods of putting a garment together; but they were quite unskilled in the administration of labor and material resources, and somewhat unskilled in that interpersonal area commonly labeled "human relations."

Authority to make decisions was far too centralized. Even the most minor issues were commonly referred to the production manager or the plant manager. Assistant supervisors were little more than bundle girls concerned with materials supply; supervisors were almost exclusively engaged in immediate direction of the day's work.

Of necessity, therefore, organizational development required, first of all, an increase in the number of supervisors, by additional appointments when necessary, but mainly by development of assistant supervisors into "real" supervisors and development of supervisors to undertake a broader range of duties. Second, it was necessary to train both supervisors and their assistants in work administration and human relations. Finally, it was necessary to increase supervisory authority by pushing downward the level at which decisions were made.

Had the full scope of these problems and the intricacies of their solution been apparent before the initial survey, measurements could have been collected for all relevant persons at all times. But any development program—the present one in particular—is a self-correcting mechanism, and the full extent of the needed correctives was not known until well into 1963. For this reason, evidence about supervisory leadership was obtained only about unit supervisors during each of the first two Weldon surveys: Limited descriptions of assistant supervisors' behavior were obtained only in 1964.

It is possible, however, to review the descriptions of unit heads made at the outset of the program, and then to trace these descriptions across two subsequent years. Comparisons may then be made to the descriptions of assistants by operators and of unit heads by assistants in 1964. Three blocks of data are available for assessing the nature of supervisory leadership at these times. One block consists of descriptions by production employees of their supervisors' performance on three aspects or dimensions of leadership. The second consists of a set of more evaluative judgments by operators of the adequacy of the supervision they received. The third block consists of retrospective descriptions in 1966 by managers, supervisors, and assistant supervisors of behavioral style changes attributable to the training seminars conducted in 1963.

The first set of data to be considered is derived from a theory of leadership, and an associated measurement method, that had previously been used in other organizations.[1] Briefly, the approach holds that there are four principal dimensions of supervisory leadership activity, and that these may be assessed for any particular supervisor by questionnaire responses of subordinates. The three indexes employed in the present study are: *Support*—the extent to which the supervisor behaves with respectful regard for subordinates' personal needs and concerns; *Goal emphasis*—the extent to which the supervisor does things to stimulate enthusiasm for the goal or the task to be done; and *Work facilitation*—the extent to which the supervisor provides the conditions and means for getting the work done. Scores on these three indexes for Weldon and Harwood supervisors, and for Weldon assistant supervisors, are shown in Figure 15–1. Several facts are discernible from this figure and are worth noting:

In 1962, the Weldon supervisors (unit heads only, not their assistant supervisors) provided to operators much less support, much less work facilitation, and slightly less goal emphasis than did their counterparts at Harwood.

By 1963, the Weldon supervisors had increased, but only slightly, their support and goal emphasis, and had decreased their provision of work facilitation. The latter change was not significant, and in any case might be attributed to the disruptive work reorganization going on at the time and to the beginning of the process for separating supervisors somewhat from direct work with production operators.

---

[1] A full account of the rationale for these measures and the empirical evidence of their validity may be found in the following source: D. G. Bowers and S. E. Seashore, "Predicting Organizational Effectiveness with a Four-Factor Theory of Leadership," *Administrative Science Quarterly*, September 1966, pp. 238–263.

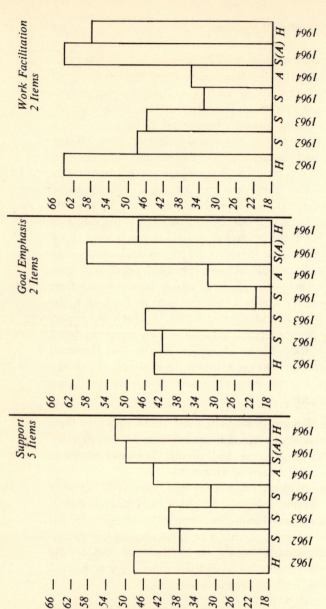

FIGURE 15–1. Leadership Description, 1962–64

N = number of respondents.
H = Harwood supervisors rated by employees (1962, N = 47; 1964, N = 46).
S = Weldon supervisors rated by employees (1962, N = 143; 1963, N = 144; and 1964, N = 111).
A = Weldon assistant supervisors rated by employees (1962, N = 143; 1963, N = 144; and 1964, N = 111).
S(A) = Weldon supervisors rated by assistant supervisors (1962, N = 143; 1963, N = 144; and 1964, N = 111).
S(A) = Weldon supervisors rated by assistant supervisors (1964, N = 13).

By 1964, it was no longer possible to have measures at Weldon comparable to those obtained in the previous years, for the reason that the roles of supervisors and of assistant supervisors had changed so much that they were no longer the same roles. Accordingly, for 1964, the measures refer not to a single relationship—supervisors to operators—but to a three-level hierarchy, with assessments by both operators and assistant supervisors of the amounts of leadership provided by the supervisors, and with a separate assessment by the operators of the leadership provided by the assistant supervisors. The figure shows that by 1964 the amount of leadership provided directly to operators by supervisors had dropped very substantially; this is in accordance with the effort to change the supervisor's role away from direct supervision and toward system management responsibilities and confirms the success of that effort. At the same time, the direct leadership provided by these supervisors to their assistant supervisors was at a relatively high level—the S(A) column—in all three leadership dimensions.

Also, at the same time, the support leadership provided to operators by the assistants was relatively high although goal emphasis and work facilitation were low. This state of affairs probably came about because during that year, goal emphasis and work facilitation were being provided very much by the engineers and consultants who were then engaged in intensive work directly with operators on the shop floor. The situation at Weldon in the fall of 1964 can thus be seen as one of incomplete transition from a state in which operators received leadership almost exclusively from the few supervisors and in moderate amounts, to a transitional state in which they received a greater total amount of leadership, but from three significant sources—the supervisors, the assistant supervisors, and the consultants and engineers. The aggregate is undoubtedly a substantial increase in leadership for the operators.

The comparison between Weldon and Harwood for 1964 (and also for 1962) is problematic, as information is lacking on the leadership provided by Harwood's few assistant supervisors. It is clear that the Harwood supervisors had increased their provision of support and goal emphasis during the two-year period and diminished slightly their provision of work facilitation. It is our belief that the aggregate amount of leadership provided to operators remains in 1964 greater at Harwood than at Weldon, even though the difference between the plants has been diminished, particularly as regards providing support to operators.

The second set of data to be considered in this connection is presented in Table 15-1, showing the responses of Weldon and Harwood operators to questions evaluating the performance of their supervisors. Here again we have the difficulty of interpretation arising from the failure to assess the behavior of assistant supervisors as well as of the unit heads. The data show that the Weldon unit supervisors between 1962 and 1964 changed toward less close supervision of operators, gave less exclusive emphasis to productivity, and became (from the operator's view) less good at dealing with people. These changes, although small, are compatible with the changing role of the unit head described earlier. During the same period, the Harwood unit supervisors, already superior on most items, became even more so.

The third set of data were obtained by administering a form constructed for that purpose on the basis of an extensive review of literature pertaining to laboratory training and its presumed effects. In January, 1966, this retrospective evaluation of the effects of sensitivity training seminars was obtained from those production managers, supervisors, and assistants who had participated. All of those original participants were still employed by the firm. Figures 15-2, 15-3, and 15-4 indicate, on fifteen semantic-differential items, participants' perceptions of themselves, their superior, and each other (peers) *before training, immediately after training,* and *at present* (January 1966). Several conclusions may be drawn:

Even at this distance in time from the training, approximately as much change is perceived to have occurred at the time of training as is perceived to have occurred in the two and a half years since then. Considered jointly, these two incre-

TABLE 15-1

COMPARISONS AND CHANGES IN RESPONSES TO SUPERVISION QUESTIONS, 1962, 1963, AND 1964

	WELDON 1962	t*	HARWOOD 1962	t*	WELDON 1963	t*	WELDON 1964	t*	HARWOOD 1964
Close or very close supervision	46%		38%		41%		27%		33%
Supervisor feels productivity most or one of most important things	85	Sig.	82	Sig.	73	Sig.	71	Sig.	83
Supervisor good or very good in dealing with people	77		62	Sig.	62	Sig.	46	Sig.	75
Supervisor good or very good in planning, organizing, and scheduling	60		51		55	Sig.	45	Sig.	87
Important or very important to supervisor to make work satisfying and interesting	55		48		56		44	Sig.	72
Considerable or great deal of unreasonable pressure from supervisor	15		11		13		11		4

NOTE: The figures show the percentages of respondents checking the two most favorable (or, in some cases, most unfavorable) of the response categories offered in the multiple-choice questionnaire. The number of Weldon respondents in 1962 was 143, 144 in 1963, and 111 in 1964. Harwood had 47 respondents in 1962 and 46 in 1964.

* The t test for the significance of the difference between means at the .05 level was used.

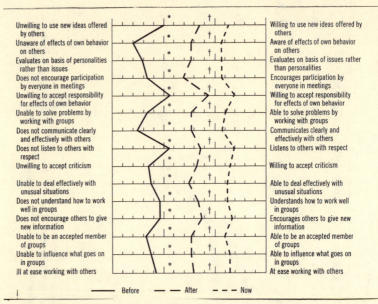

Unwilling to use new ideas offered by others	Willing to use new ideas offered by others
Unaware of effects of own behavior on others	Aware of effects of own behavior on others
Evaluates on basis of personalities rather than issues	Evaluates on basis of issues rather than personalities
Does not encourage participation by everyone in meetings	Encourages participation by everyone in meetings
Unwilling to accept responsibility for effects of own behavior	Willing to accept responsibility for effects of own behavior
Unable to solve problems by working with groups	Able to solve problems by working with groups
Does not communicate clearly and effectively with others	Communicates clearly and effectively with others
Does not listen to others with respect	Listens to others with respect
Unwilling to accept criticism	Willing to accept criticism
Unable to deal effectively with unusual situations	Able to deal effectively with unusual situations
Does not understand how to work well in groups	Understands how to work well in groups
Does not encourage others to give new information	Encourages others to give new information
Unable to be an accepted member of groups	Able to be an accepted member of groups
Unable to influence what goes on in groups	Able to influence what goes on in groups
Ill at ease working with others	At ease working with others

———— Before ——— After – – – Now

FIGURE 15–2. Perceptions in January 1966 of Behavioral Change from Before Training Seminars to Period Immediately After and to Time of Rating, Self-Rating

* Significant difference between Before and After measures at .05 level.

† Significant difference between After and Now measures at .05 level.

ments of change suggest that there was an initial, "sudden" change following the training seminars (a fact which coincides quite well with the impact upon operator earnings discussed in Chapter 14), and further gradual change in the subsequent months. The sometimes perplexing, seldom-answered question among proponents of this form of training, i.e., "Does change, when it results, occur immediately or only gradually over a long period of time?" would appear to be answered here. Change, or development, takes place in both ways.

Although the amount of change varies from item to item, almost all of the changes are statistically significant. Greatest changes would appear to have occurred, however, in interpersonal communication, in willingness to accept criticism, in

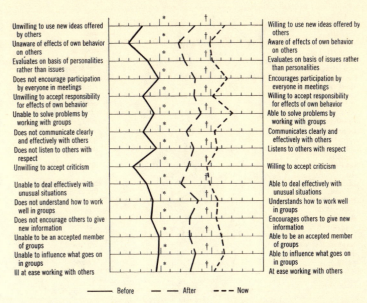

Unwilling to use new ideas offered by others	Willing to use new ideas offered by others
Unaware of effects of own behavior on others	Aware of effects of own behavior on others
Evaluates on basis of personalities rather than issues	Evaluates on basis of issues rather than personalities
Does not encourage participation by everyone in meetings	Encourages participation by everyone in meetings
Unwilling to accept responsibility for effects of own behavior	Willing to accept responsibility for effects of own behavior
Unable to solve problems by working with groups	Able to solve problems by working with groups
Does not communicate clearly and effectively with others	Communicates clearly and effectively with others
Does not listen to others with respect	Listens to others with respect
Unwilling to accept criticism	Willing to accept criticism
Unable to deal effectively with unusual situations	Able to deal effectively with unusual situations
Does not understand how to work well in groups	Understands how to work well in groups
Does not encourage others to give new information	Encourages others to give new information
Unable to be an accepted member of groups	Able to be an accepted member of groups
Unable to influence what goes on in groups	Able to influence what goes on in groups
Ill at ease working with others	At ease working with others

——— Before   — — After   - - - Now

FIGURE 15–3. Perceptions in January 1966 of Behavioral Change from Before Training Seminars to Period Immediately After and to Time of Rating, Supervisor Rating

* Significant difference between Before and After measures at .05 level.

† Significant difference between After and Now measures at .05 level.

an awareness of the effects of one's own behavior upon others, and in a willingness to use new ideas. Least change, although still sizable and significant, apparently occurred in more "active" attributes, such as understanding how to work well in groups, in ways of encouraging others to give new information, and the like.

Although absolute scale placements for self, superior, and peers differ, comparative changes are almost identical.

If only a self-description had been presented, perceptions of progress could simply reflect reduction in dissonance (i.e., so much effort on the respondent's part in training and relearning leads him to feel some progress *must* have been made by him). The fact that perceptions of peers and superiors

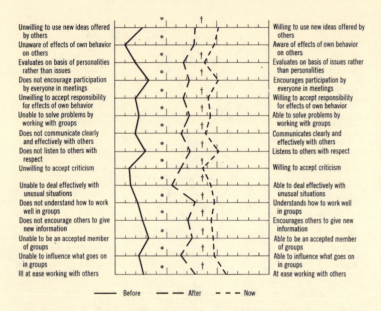

Unwilling to use new ideas offered by others		Willing to use new ideas offered by others
Unaware of effects of own behavior on others		Aware of effects of own behavior on others
Evaluates on basis of personalities rather than issues		Evaluates on basis of issues rather than personalities
Does not encourage participation by everyone in meetings		Encourages participation by everyone in meetings
Unwilling to accept responsibility for effects of own behavior		Willing to accept responsibility for effects of own behavior
Unable to solve problems by working with groups		Able to solve problems by working with groups
Does not communicate clearly and effectively with others		Communicates clearly and effectively with others
Does not listen to others with respect		Listens to others with respect
Unwilling to accept criticism		Willing to accept criticism
Unable to deal effectively with unusual situations		Able to deal effectively with unusual situations
Does not understand how to work well in groups		Understands how to work well in groups
Does not encourage others to give new information		Encourages others to give new information
Unable to be an accepted member of groups		Able to be an accepted member of groups
Unable to influence what goes on in groups		Able to influence what goes on in groups
Ill at ease working with others		At ease working with others

—— Before   — — After   - - - Now

FIGURE 15–4. Perceptions in January 1966 of Behavioral Change from Before Training Seminars to Period Immediately After and to Time of Rating, Peer Rating

* Significant difference between Before and After measures at .05 level.

† Significant difference between After and Now measures at .05 level.

are almost identical to those of self strongly reduces the likelihood of this as a sufficient explanation.

Our summary conclusions from these complex and incomplete sets of data are that: (1) Weldon operators experienced between 1962 and 1964 an increase in the total amount of leadership they received in all three dimensions of leadership; (2) this leadership increment was accompanied by a shift from a single source (the unit supervisor) to multiple sources (supervisors, assistants, and engineers); (3) these changes in amount and source of leadership are compatible with the new philosophy at Weldon and reflect some success in modification of the Weldon organizational system; and (4) these changes are fairly widely recognized by the participants, especially in areas of interpersonal communications.

Organizational Control

One aim of the Weldon change program was to alter the control structure of the organization in such a way that there would be a greater total amount of control and particularly an increase in the control exercised by people at lower ranks in the organization. "Control," in this context, refers to the purposeful exercise of influence on the activities within the organization. In this sense, control arises from both receiving and sending influence among people whose work needs to be integrated, and is generated in increased amounts by participative practices in decision-making, by increased flow of information throughout an organization, and (seemingly a paradox) by increased autonomy for individuals at lower ranks within their various areas of responsibility.

The concept of "control," and the relationship of both the amount and distribution of control to organizational effectiveness, has been explored by Tannenbaum and his colleagues.[2] Their findings suggest that a relatively large amount of total control is often associated with organizational effectiveness, and that a relatively "flat" distribution of control—i.e., not concentrated unduly in one or two top levels of the hierarchy —favors good organizational results. Their work also provides a simple and reasonably adequate method for assessing control in an organization by means of descriptive ratings obtained from members of an organization. We adopted for this study the concepts and methods developed by Tannenbaum. The results for both Weldon and Harwood for the period of this study are shown in Figure 15–5.

This figure shows that the control structure at Weldon did

[2] C. G. Smith and A. S. Tannenbaum, "Organizational Control Structure: A Comparative Analysis," *Human Relations*, November 1963, pp. 299–316. Also, A. S. Tannenbaum, "Control in Organization: Individual Adjustment and Organizational Performance," *Administrative Science Quarterly*, September 1962, pp. 236–257.

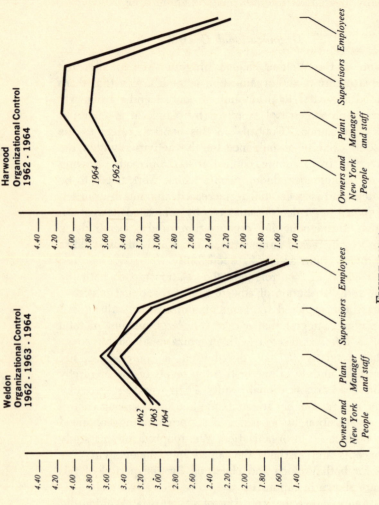

FIGURE 15–5.

Number of respondents: Weldon: 143 in 1962, 144 in 1963, and 111 in 1964. Harwood: 47 in 1962 and 46 in 1964.

NOTE: This chart represents the amount of say or influence perceived by Weldon and Harwood employees from the four hierarchical levels. High on the scale = great influence.

not change much, as seen by the employees, during the period of study; the influence of higher-level people is diminished slightly, and that of lower-level people is increased slightly, but these changes are not statistically significant; and the total amount of control (area under the curves) remains almost constant. During the same period, Harwood shows both a higher and flatter curve, and the total amount of control increased between 1962 and 1964.

The conclusion from this evidence is that the Weldon program did not achieve its objectives in this respect within the period of study even though trends of the intended kind began to appear. One may speculate that the main effects of the control program may appear much later to the nonsupervisory people than to those more immediately involved in management and supervision. This view is supported by the information on control as seen by the managers and supervisors, presented in the next section.

The Management System

The key effort to assess changes in Weldon's philosophy and practice of management was carried out with the aid of a special rating procedure designed for use in assessing and comparing organizations. Earlier we gave a brief description of the rationale and methods.[3] The rating form itself, as modified for use in the Weldon-Harwood study, consists of rating scales designed to provide descriptive ratings on 43 dimensions of organizational functioning, grouped into seven topical areas. The scales are defined in terms referring to an organization's adherence to one of four "types" (actually a continuum) of managerial systems: "System 1" (exploitative-authoritative), "System 2" (benevolent-authoritative), "System 3" (consultative), or "System 4" (participative group) philosophy of man-

---

[3] For a more complete discussion of the theory and the use of this instrument, see R. Likert, *New Patterns of Management*, New York, McGraw-Hill, 1961, Chap. 14; and *The Human Organization: Its Management and Values*, also by Likert, New York, McGraw-Hill, 1967.

agement. These types of managerial systems are further defined as follows:

System 1

This management system assumes that labor is largely a market commodity, with time freely sold and purchased. It conceives of the manager's job as consisting of *decision, direction*, and *surveillance*, relies primarily upon coercion as a motivating force, and makes little or no provision for the effects of human emotion and interdependence. As a result, communication in this system is sluggish, largely downward in direction, and frequently distorted. Goals are established and decisions made by top management only, based upon fragmentary, often inaccurate and inadequate information. This produces disparity between the desires and interests of the members and the goals of the organization. For these reasons, only high levels of the organization feel any real responsibility for the attainment of established objectives. Their reliance upon coercion as a motivating force leads to an almost total absence of cooperative teamwork and mutual influence and to a quite low true ability of superiors to exercise control in the work situation. Dissatisfaction is prevalent, with sub-servient attitudes toward superiors, hostility toward peers, and contempt for subordinates. Performance is usually mediocre, with high costs, excessive absence, and substantial manpower turnover. Quality is maintained only by extensive surveillance and a great deal of rework.

System 2

This management system assumes that labor is a market commodity, but an imperfect one: Once purchased, it is susceptible to periodic emotional and interpersonal "inter-ferences." Consequently, to *decision, direction*, and *surveil-lance* it adds a fourth managerial duty: expurgating the annoying affect of subordinate members. This fact permits some small amount of upward and lateral communication, although most is downward, and sizable distortion usually exists. Policies are established and basic decisions made by upper management, sometimes with opportunity for comment from subordinate supervisory levels. Some minor implementa-tion decisions may be made at lower levels, but only within the carefully prescribed limits set by the top echelon. Managerial personnel, therefore, usually feel responsibility for attaining the assigned objectives, whereas rank-and-file members usually feel little or none. Very little cooperative teamwork exists, and superiors at lower echelons are able to exercise only moderate true control in the work situation. Attitudes toward superiors are subservient, and hostility is prevalent toward peers, but the absence of open contempt toward subordinates makes dissatisfaction less intense. Performance may be fair to good, although high costs, absence, and manpower turnover frequently occur.

System 3

This management system does not assume labor to be a market commodity. It still reserves to the manager the tasks of *decision,* and *direction,* but removes *surveillance* as a major function. Little recourse to coercion occurs. In their places recognition of the frequently disruptive effects of human emotion is expanded to include employee involvement through consultation. This practice encourages a moderate amount of valid upward communication, although lateral communication is limited by the prevalence of man-to-man, rather than group, decision-making. Communication is, therefore, usually accurate and only occasionally distorted. In line with this, broad policy decisions are made at the top, but specific objectives to implement these policies are entrusted to lower managers for consultative decision-making. For all these reasons, a substantial proportion of the members of the organization feel responsible for attaining established objectives, and the system makes use of most positive motivational forces, except those which would otherwise arise from group processes. Some dissatisfaction may exist, but normally satisfaction is moderately high, with only some degree of hostility expressed toward peers, some condescension toward subordinates. Performance is ordinarily good; costs, absence, and turnover moderate; and quality problems no cause for major concern.

System 4

This management system assumes that employees are essential parts of an organizational structure which has been built at great cost and necessarily maintained with the same attention and care given more tangible assets. It conceives of decision as a process, rather than a prerogative, with the manager's responsibility consisting, not of himself deciding, but of making sure that the best possible decisions result. In this light, he focuses his efforts upon building an overlapping structure of cohesive, highly motivated, participative groups, coordinated by multiple memberships. Within this highly coordinated and motivated system, characterized by high mutual confidence and trust, communication is adequate, rapid and accurate. Because goals are established and decisions made with the participation of all those affected, objectives are comparatively closely aligned with the needs and interests of all members, and all motivational forces push in the direction of obtaining the established objectives. The closely knit system in addition permits superiors and subordinates alike to exercise great control over the work situation. Employees at all levels are highly satisfied, but without complacency, and feel great reciprocal respect and trust. Performance is very good; costs, absence and turnover are low; and high quality is the natural concern of all.

This instrument was completed in 1964 by all top plant managers, supervisors, and assistant supervisors at both Weldon and at the Harwood comparison plant. Those at the Weldon plant completed the form three times—once to describe the preacquisition situation, another time to describe the then present situation, and a third time to describe the ideal situation. Only "now" and "ideal" ratings were obtained at Harwood. The preacquisition Weldon situation was also judged independently by the research team shortly before the other ratings were collected, on the basis of earlier conversations and observations. Still another rating of Weldon was obtained by content coding the nondirective interview and questionnaire survey materials collected in 1962.

Figure 15–6 shows the results for Weldon, based upon the views of managers, supervisors, and assistant supervisors in that plant. These ratings were all obtained in the fall of 1964, but refer to the past ("How things were at Weldon, as you recall them, at the time of acquisition"), and to the future

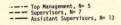

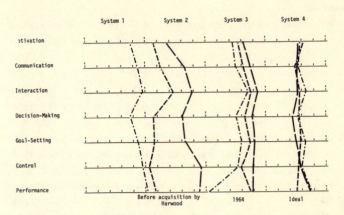

FIGURE 15–6. Weldon's Progress Toward Participative Management*

* Based on anonymous ratings by 25 Weldon managers and supervisors using R. Likert's 43-factor "Profile of Organizational and Performance Characteristics" (in *New Patterns of Management*, New York, McGraw-Hill, 1961). System 1 is "exploitive, coercive, authoritative"; System 2 is "benevolent authoritative"; System 3 is "consultative"; and System 4 is a "participative, group-based" organizational system. Achievement of System 4 was desired by both owners and members.

("Ideally, how would you like things to be at Weldon") as well as to the then present time ("How things are now at Weldon").

There was a general consensus among the three groups of Weldon raters that Weldon, before acquisition, fell at the borderline between the "exploitative-authoritative" and "benevolent-authoritative" systems. The ratings for "now" (1964) indicate that Weldon had shifted to System 3, the "consultative" type. The raters all shared the desire to move further to System 4, the "participative" system. There is a high degree of type consistency for each of these sets of ratings; variation is ordinarily within a given "type" classification, seldom across types.[4] In addition, there is a remarkable agreement among raters about what the state of affairs at Weldon was, is, and should be.

With respect to the recalled state of Weldon before acquisition, the organization was then clearly at the borderline between the exploitative-authoritative and the benevolent-authoritative types. The judgment of top plant management people, who certainly were least hesitant about expressing their honest opinion (but who may also have been the most accurate in estimating the researchers' own view), was that Weldon was frankly exploitative. Supervisors and assistant supervisors, on the other hand, described preacquisition Weldon as more benevolent. The ratings by the research team observers, and ratings from the recorded interview and questionnaire material gathered at the time (1962) are less liable to recall distortion; these ratings placed Weldon in 1962 also at the borderline between the two types, with results only slightly more favorable than those provided by the plant top managers. Even with allowance for difference in personal experience arising from rank and from errors of recall, it seems reasonably certain that Weldon, before acquisition, was seen by Weldon people as an authoritative and occasionally exploitative system.

By the fall of 1964, when these ratings were obtained, Weldon supervisory and managerial people saw their organization as having moved to the "consultative" position on the type scale. By then managers and supervisors were much more in agreement in their views, although the rank differences still persisted. At this time also the observers' ratings (not shown in Figure 15–6) were similar to those made by the Weldon people themselves.

With respect to the desired state of affairs, there was a

---

[4] Extensive, unpublished factor analyses of data collected from a number of organizations indicate that "halo effects" cannot account for this within-profile consistency. Systemically different organizations produce a large single factor representing the scale of "types" while systemically similar organizations produce approximately twelve factors, all interpretable within Likert's conceptual scheme.

remarkable agreement among all the Weldon raters, regardless
of rank, that they wished to progress further to a fully participative system. While some allowance should be made for the
fact that these ratings were constructed at a time when there
was considerable effort to advocate participative principles,
the ratings at least indicate an acceptance of participation
as an ideal.

The results for Harwood for the same period are shown in
Figure 15–7. In the fall of 1964, the Harwood people, with
high consensus, described their organization as having the
characteristics of a moderately participative system. Like the
Weldon people, they desired to move further toward participative practices.

At this point, we can introduce information from a time
subsequent to the period of study with which we are mainly
concerned. The research team, and the new Weldon owners,

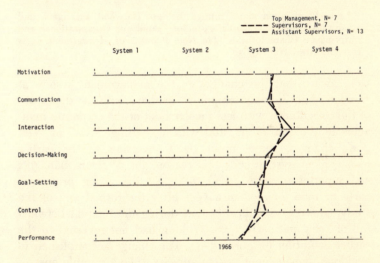

FIGURE 15–7. Weldon's 1966 Profile of Organizational Characteristics*

* Based on anonymous ratings of 27 Weldon managers and super-
visors using R. Likert's 43-factor "Profile of Organizational and
Performance Characteristics" (in *New Patterns of Management*, New
York, McGraw-Hill, 1961).

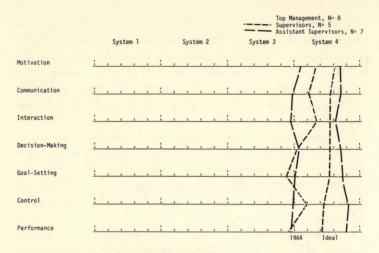

FIGURE 15–8. Harwood's Participative Management*

* Based on anonymous ratings by 20 Harwood managers and supervisors using R. Likert's 43-factor "Profile of Organizational and Performance Characteristics" (in *New Patterns of Management*, New York, McGraw-Hill, 1961).

were aware that the changes in the management system at Weldon might be only temporary; perhaps with the departure of the consultants, with less involvement of the corporate managers in Weldon affairs, and with a "settling down" of Weldon's changes, there might be a reversion to the earlier management system. For this reason, the Weldon managers and supervisors were asked to repeat the rating procedure early in 1966, more than a year after the formal end of the study. The results indicated that during the interval between fall of 1964 and early 1966, Weldon had not reverted to the earlier condition (Figure 15–8). The change accomplished in Weldon's management system appears to be a durable one.

Summary

The aim of this chapter has been to provide evidence and to draw conclusions about the success of Weldon's program in changing the management philosophy of the organization and in changing the ways in which the organization functions. Seen as a whole, the evidence is incomplete, open to other interpretations. Nevertheless, there is support for the assertion that Weldon did indeed change, and in intended ways:

Supervisory leadership at Weldon, as experienced by the production employees, became greater in amount and shifted from leadership exclusively from the unit heads and the production manager to leadership from multiple sources. Role changes came about that reduced the direct leadership exercised by the supervisors, who became more involved in work system management, less involved in direct supervision; these supervisors, in their new role, were perceived by employees more favorably in some respects, less favorably in others. At the same time, the assistant supervisors' role grew in its importance to the employees as they were permitted and encouraged to take over significant leadership activities on the shop floor. During the change period (although direct evidence is lacking) a serious leadership deficiency was filled in part by the input of consultant and staff leadership on a temporary, transitional basis. Program goals were thus partly achieved. Effective leadership became greater in amount and more rationally dispersed in different, related leadership roles. The change in supervisory leadership was still incomplete at the end of the study period.

The changes in the control structure of the Weldon organization were not sufficient to be apparent to the nonsupervisory people. Such minor changes as did occur were of kinds intended, but they were very small. It may be that more time is required before major changes, affecting the lower ranks of such an organization, can be brought about.

Global assessments of the Weldon management system, as seen by the participants and confirmed by the research observers, indicate that a radical transformation was accomplished. In all major areas of managerial activity, Weldon shifted from an authoritative (and in some ways an exploitative) system, to one based upon consultative values and principles. An ideal of further change toward participative principles was implanted, and during the year following the change program, Weldon continued to progress toward its own adopted ideal form of management system. This change—the major one sought—appears to have been brought about in a context that makes it a stable new condition.

16

IMPLICATIONS FOR MANAGING ORGANIZATIONAL CHANGE

David G. Bowers and Stanley E. Seashore

A STORY OF success or failure in management practice has only passing interest, and little utility, unless there can be derived from it some ideas for general application. These derived ideas may be of two kinds. Some have their value in the shorter run, and consist of suggestions, examples, and rules of thumb that may guide a manager (or a researcher) in his current work. Some derived ideas have the greater value in the long run, and consist of conclusions, often abstract and tentative, that help to build workable general theories about the management of organizations. A case can help by showing that some terms and concepts for describing events are more realistic than others that might be used. A case can reveal fatal flaws in the assumptions a manager is living by. A case can reveal some of the interplay of factors that produces an outcome—good or bad—and can thus lead to a significant shift in emphasis among familiar ideas.

The problem lies in drawing from the specific case some conclusions of a general kind that will help one to understand and better to control the course of events in other and future situations. It is an obligation for those who report cases to suggest how they bear on current developments in theory and practice relating to organizational management. This chapter undertakes the task. We shall summarize the main concepts we used in interpreting the Weldon case and suggest their roots in the work of others. We shall comment upon the meaning of the Weldon events for those concerned with making or understanding organizational changes. We shall comment also on a number of issues that are raised or emphasized by the Weldon case, but for which we have, from this one case alone, no very useful interpretations to suggest.

General Orientation

A main theme in the current development of theory about human organizations is implicit in the term "sociotechnical system." This term conveys much of our orientation to the Weldon case. It implies a concern with both social and technical factors at the same time. It implies a concern with the system properties and new systemic processes that are generated when people interact with one another and with their work. It implies a relatively minor concern about individual reactions and changes except as these help to understand the system.

The concept of "system" is both old and new. Modern general systems theory, stemming largely from the study of smaller biological entities, offers ideas that illuminate the workings of large organizations. One theme from this source, for example, is the self-evident but unappreciated one that all parts of a system are interdependent. A change in any one part or subsystem requires adaptive changes in other parts. It is our view that managers will profit greatly from viewing their organizations as if they were living systems, not as relatively simple physical systems with buffered parts and replaceable subsystems. It is useful to consider that work arrangements are related to the associated human organization in most intimate ways, such that the performance characteristics of the technological system are instantly modified by changing characteristics of the social system and in turn require adaptations in the social arrangements. Similarly, within the social subsystem alone, any attempt to alter some part—say, for example, the norms and values governing compensation—will surely interact with other parts and demand accommodating changes of many kinds.

Translated into a precept, this fact of systemic interdependence implies, among other things, that managerial policies and programs of limited scope—i.e., relevant to only one part of the organization or of its work environment—are no longer good enough. Policies and programs must possess the quality of a coherent whole and must refer to the whole of the organizational system and its related technical system as well as its environment. Fads and fancies, tricks and gimmicks, become more suspect than ever, however well clothed they may be in their own limited and often elegant logic. Management training programs have often been ineffective, not because they were "bad" training programs, but because they were not integrated with other aspects of the total organizational system. Computerized operations control, programed product innovations, "improved" cost accounting systems, to name some respectable examples, gain their merit and utility in large part from the coherence of the sociotechnical system of which they become a part. They fail, usually, when introduced with insufficient regard for the establishment of a wide network of new and modified system interdependencies of kinds necessary for the innovation to have a "place" in the whole.

These remarks about the interdependence of parts in systems serve only to illustrate in an elementary way the relevance of general systems theory to the understanding of sociotechnical systems. A recent book by Katz and Kahn treats extensively and in depth the systemic nature of human organizations.[1] Further guides to general systems theory and refer-

---

[1] D. Katz and R. L. Kahn, *Social Psychology of Organizations*, New York, John Wiley, 1966.

ences to other sources can be found in the *General Systems Yearbook*.[2]

The term "sociotechnical system" refers to a unit of analysis that embraces both the human organization and its related technology; the latter includes not only the physical facilities, materials, machines, and the like, but also the arrangements for information generation and control, the plan for work flow, the standards for controlling the quality or pace of work operations, and the like. It is not at all clear where the "human" leaves off and where the "technical" begins; many of the vital elements of a coherent technical system have little or no physical existence (e.g., quality standards, work-pace norms, customs about information exchange, beliefs about customer demands, etc.); and, on the other hand, some of the vital features of the human organization are fixed by physical elements of work space, instrumentation of work places, and the like. The distinction between "technical" and "social" is rather arbitrary, although for many purposes it is useful to make the distinction. The systems are "open," composed in turn of subsystems, and related to form larger identifiable systems. The boundaries between them are marked not only by separation, but by vital transactions and interdependences.

The label "sociotechnical" is used here to emphasize our interest in the transactions and interdependences which are too often overlooked in management planning. Its counterpart in a more familiar and more advanced field goes by the name "man-machine system" and carries with it the notions of considering the system as a whole, of designing machines and controls with consideration for the demands placed upon operators, and for the range of performance capacities that reasonably can be expected in an operator. Or, alternatively, the term suggests getting unusual operators, by selection or training, who are capable of acting effectively within the given machine characteristics under a wide variety of operating conditions.

---

[2] See *General Systems Yearbook*, published by the Society for the Advancement of General Systems Theory.

At the level of a total manufacturing activity, similar considerations also apply. A factory technology is no better in use than the social system that is to join with it; it is difficult to create and sustain an adequate social system if the technology is faulty or inappropriate to the available human resources. Weldon's initial new production unit—Unit III—provides an example. The plan for the unit was neat and rational, well provided with physical requirements, but failed during many months to pay off, for want of an integrated system of relationships between persons and between persons and their jobs. A sound technology was not sufficient in itself to assure good performance for this unit as a whole.

One significant conclusion from these views of the relationships between the social and technical aspects of a factory is that they preclude any confident judgment about the goodness of either a social system or a technical system apart from their suitability for each other and apart from their total system effectiveness.[3]

The goodness of any particular form of social organization, and of any particular set of guiding principles for social process, lies not so much in its own inherent merit as in its utility for effective use of work facilities and work process resources. It is often asserted that some forms of organizational life are better than others; people argue for a "participative" organizational life, or for a return to a centrally managed work system with individual incentives to assure performance of the system as a whole; others argue for still other ideas. It is our view (in strictly utilitarian terms, apart from ethical or humanitarian considerations) that if some forms of organiza-

---

[3] See M. D. Kilbridge, "Reduced Costs Through Job Enlargement: A Case," *Journal of Business, University of Chicago,* October, 1960, for a good example, in which a household equipment manufacturer found it desirable to abandon a superbly designed assembly technology, reverting to a more "primitive" technology in order to have the cost and quality gains from greater sophistication in the social system. See also A. S. Tannenbaum, *The Social Psychology of Work Organizations,* Belmont, Cal., Wadsworth Publishing Co., 1966, for an account of studies illustrating the interdependence of social and technological aspects of work.

tional life can be said to be generally better than others it is only because there is a prevailing set of common unresolved problems shared by many organizations. From this view we can and do propose that an emphasis on participative principles in management, and an emphasis upon employee development, are particularly "good" for many organizations at the present time for the reason that these facilitate the integration of the human organization with a technology that becomes more complex, more insulated from effective central control, more dependent upon local coordination and upon self-management. The test of competing emphases in the structure and functioning of human organizations lies in the results they produce for the total sociotechnical system.

Thus, the key ideas behind the Weldon conversion program, while still somewhat novel were thought to be—and proved to be—appropriate for an organization faced with a need to adapt quickly to a moderate change in its business environment. The previous organizational arrangements were incapable of eliciting the motives, the skills, and the coordinative efforts and measures demanded by even modest stress, and its performance became even worse in the frenzy of effort to cope with the situation without modification of itself.

The key ideas about organizational structure and organizational process embodied in the Weldon program are not really very "advanced" or "experimental" but merely well chosen and applied. There are still other variations in organizational theory that are more advanced, more complicated, more problematic, and probably more useful in relation to the kinds of performances that will be required of business and industrial organizations in the future. Some examples of such lines of thought and practice can be seen in the work of Eric Trist and his colleagues at the Tavistock Institute, London, on the problems of adapting organizations to economic and social environments of multiplying complexity;[4] in the work of Warren

---

[4] E. L. Trist, *et al.*, *Organizational Choice*, London, Tavistock Publications, 1963. F. E. Emery and E. L. Trist, "Socio-technical systems," in C. W. Churchman and M. Verhulst (eds.) *Management Sciences*,

Bennis[5] and others in connection with increasing demands placed on the information-generating and information-using capabilities of organizations; and in the work of Rensis Likert[6] who envisions a universally applicable continuously adaptive organizational system. Abraham Maslow comments on ways of accommodating authoritarian personalities within a dominantly nonauthoritarian organization.[7]

The Weldon case illustrates on a small scale the realistic possibility of making rational, informed, and conscious choices in managerial strategy, as contrasted with making choices restricted on habitual, traditional, or normative grounds. The range of possibilities for managers is much greater than that normally considered available.

A third feature of our general orientation to the Weldon case and emerging organizational theory relates to the issues of management of change. It is trite to note the accelerating pace of technological and social change; the pace is already taking on the qualities of a nightmare. We need to have better ideas about how to plan and expedite change, how to keep it from becoming disruptive and nearly fatal as in the Weldon case before the conversion program.

The Weldon case reaffirms the view of organizational and social change advanced by Kurt Lewin some years ago.[8] Systems of social roles, with their associated patterns of attitudes, expectations, and behavior norms, share with biological systems the characteristic of homeostasis—i.e., tendencies to

---

Models and Techniques, Oxford, Pergamon Press, 1960. H. Perlmutter, *On the Building of Viable Institutions*, London, Tavistock Publications, 1965. F. E. Emery and E. L. Trist, "The Causal Texture of Organizational Environments," *Human Relations*, February 1965, pp. 21–32.

[5] W. Bennis, "Toward a 'Truly' Scientific Management: The Concept of Organizational Health," *Industrial Management Review*, Number 1, (Fall) 1962.

[6] R. Likert, *New Patterns of Management*, New York, McGraw-Hill, 1961.

[7] A. Maslow, *Summer Notes on Social Psychology of Industry and Management*, Delmar, Cal., Non-Linear Systems, Inc., 1962.

[8] K. Lewin, *Field Theory in Social Science*, New York, Harper & Row, 1951.

resist change, to restore the previous state after a disturbance. In observing instances of successful change, Lewin noted that they had three phases: first, an "unfreezing" or disruption of the initial steady state, then a period of disturbance with trial of various adaptive possibilities, and finally a period of consolidation of change with a "refreezing" in a new steady state.

The Weldon organization was unable, even in the face of severe distress, to become released from the rigidities of its past, to unfreeze itself. Heroic measures were needed to create enough disturbance to allow normal change processes to begin within the organization. These unfreezing events— sensitivity training, for example, and reorganization of the work processes—were imposed from external sources. These steps were needed even though the key people within the Weldon organization were well aware of the need for change, discussed it constantly, and were largely in agreement (although superficially) about the kinds of changes they desired.

One might observe that an imposed unfreezing process carries with it the risk of permanent damage to the organization, and the possibility of total destruction. In this context, one can see the essential function of providing a supportive element during the change process. A number of the elements in the Weldon conversion program no doubt had their effect through the provision of assurance that some features of the situation, at least, were dependable. The early efforts to convey to Weldon people an image of the desired end-state, and visits to Harwood to see such a state in reality, no doubt had their effects later by providing a cognitive framework within which emotional, nonrational stresses of transition could be contained. Similarly, the refusal of the management to yield to the temptation to be secretive about change plans no doubt served to sustain confidence during periods of stress.

The refreezing of Weldon in a new and more effective state is not regarded as a permanent thing, but as another stage in the evolution and continuous adaptation of the organization. Some features of the conversion program explicitly include the provision of built-in capacities for easier changes in the future.

Why Weldon Succeeded

Weldon is not unique in the history of organizational change and development. Many organizations have changed as much or more and have improved their performance characteristics even more dramatically. Those who review the available reports of purposeful change, nevertheless, are likely to be impressed by the difficulties and great costs ordinarily associated with organizational change. Many organizations fail entirely to alter their capacity to function unless aided by extreme stress that compels change, or unless the change is associated with social revolution—the replacement of key people in relatively large numbers. Many managers have been impressed by the long time required to bring about change, and by the tendency of an organization to revert to its earlier conditions. It is sobering to reflect on how limited is our confident knowledge of optimum change strategies and methods.

Weldon is an instance of substantial, although partial, success in achieving planned organizational change goals in a relatively short time, with relatively little manpower wastage, and with a reasonable expectation that the changes will be permanent, self-sustaining. There are two main themes in our view of the reasons for Weldon's success: (1) A multiplicity of varied change strategies and methods was employed, and (2) there was unusual scope and coherence in the program of change. These themes stem in part from observations of the events that took place, and in part from the conceptual views outlined in the preceeding pages, where we argued that systemic considerations often defeat narrowly based efforts to improve organizations. These two themes are illustrated not only in the modification of Weldon's social system, but also in the changed behavior of the individuals who make up the organization and in whose behavior the social system is expressed.

Individual Change

There are four general approaches that may be taken by managers whose aim is to improve the performance of individuals.

They may take as a method the alteration of the individual's work environment in ways that will induce behavior changes or in ways that give better results for the same behavior; the ways to do this are familiar, as in the case of redesigning jobs, providing improved physical facilities or equipment, reallocating authority, improving work flow, and the like. A second approach to individual behavior change is to alter the perceptions and cognitions of people, perhaps through informational training programs, discussion, persuasion, and propaganda intended to improve the clarity, veridicality, or relevance of the individuals' views of their work situation. Still a third approach is to try directly to alter the motivation of individuals, perhaps by changing the incentive system, by invoking group processes in goal-setting, by direct threat and pressure, and the like. Finally, there is the approach based upon implanting new skills and habits by direct instruction, coaching, example, and practice.

It seems unlikely that any one of these alone will have much effect upon individual behavior within the normal range of organizational conditions, or that the effects will be stable. The failure of many company information programs and the frequent failure of incentive pay systems illustrate the point. An effective change program at the individual level is likely to call upon several, if not all, of these different and complementary approaches.

The Weldon program attempted to adopt multiple targets and methods in the effort to improve permanently the performance of individuals within the organization. Technical changes in jobs were accompanied by skill training, guided practice, revised incentive rates, persuasive efforts. The conversion to use of group and consultative processes in shop-floor management was carried out by a combination of explicit policy change, skill instruction and practice for supervisors, demonstration of the methods by higher-level managers, propaganda, and rewards for success. While there appear in retrospect many instances of partial effort and partial success in the Weldon case, it is to be noted that, in most instances, the individual employee experienced a multiplicity of consistent

forces—situational, cognitive, motivational, and behavioral—
that encouraged him to try and then to adopt for himself new
patterns of behavior at work.

Social System Change

It is not enough to alter individual behavior within an organization if the characteristics of the organization are incompat-
ible with the intended new behavior, or if they are irrelevant
to it. There must be a relationship between the intended
patterns of individual behavior and the intended features of
the organizational system so that they are mutually supportive.
In addition, the social system itself must be internally coherent, with elements that are compatible. During a period of
organizational change, stresses are likely to be created when
some parts of a social system are altered without corresponding
adaptations in other parts; and these stresses probably have
the effect of forcing ultimate convergence upon (or reversion
to) a "type" of system that is initially dominant in the system
elements, or the "type" that is most primitive in the sense of
allowing individualistic, competitive, authoritative values to
dominate unduly over organizational, collaborative, and voluntaristic values.

In this view, the original Weldon social organization was a
rather "primitive" one, although not a simple one, and the
successful change of such an organization to a more "advanced" state would require the simultaneous and consistent
modification of many of its features. The Weldon change
program did in fact advance in several ways at the same time.
The environment of the organization was substantially altered
by the fact of take-over and the availability of ready capital;
the new ownership began early to advocate a "philosophy"—a
set of guiding values and assumptions—that was distinctly
different from that prevailing in the past; structural changes
in the formal organization were introduced in ways incom-
patible with the old system and compatible with the proposed
new philosophy: organizational processes were introduced
that were unworkable under the old system and supportive

of the new. In these several ways the Weldon organization began to take on a new form (e.g., more supervisors, an additional level in the hierarchy, additional staff roles, etc.), a new set of processes for sustaining organizational life (e.g., consultative procedures in decision-making, group processes in coordination, enlargement of the information and communication activities, etc.), and a new set of beliefs and values (e.g., that individuals can and should behave responsibly, that personal and organizational goals can be compatible, that control may be widely shared without risk of anarchy, etc.). As in the case of the approach to individual change, Weldon's approach to social system change involved multiple strategies, multiple change targets, and compatibility among the new system elements.

Linking Technical and Social Change

The idea of an integrated program of social and technical change was expressed in the Weldon case in only limited and faltering ways, partly for lack of early and explicit planning in this area and partly because engineers and work systems people, and their counterparts in general management and in social technology, are not accustomed to this form of collaboration. The linkage of the two was actually accomplished primarily by the new owners, who alone were in a position to insure some balance and coordination among the various elements of the program. Nevertheless, some significant events and procedures reflect the view that the social organization of a factory must be not merely compatible with, but integral with, the system of work roles and the systems for operations control.

In concrete application, the concept of a "sociotechnical system" implies that technological changes, however small, must be carried out, not only with reference to the logic of work technology, but equally with reference to the potentials of the social situation and the possibility that the change can itself contribute to the modification and the strengthening of the social system. In the Weldon case, technical changes of considerable scope were initiated early in the program and continued at a good pace for the duration of the program. No doubt the imposed upheaval of the physical layout and work flow contributed to the general change process by destroying the physical basis for continuing old relationships and by providing an atmosphere in which further changes were to be expected. More specifically, however, there were instances of coordination of a more purposeful kind. The division of the plant into units, for example, was not only compatible with the intended new organizational form and process but served to help activate it by stabilizing jobs, making more of the performance variance controllable by the people within a unit, providing a clearer and more comprehensible common task for the members of a unit, and by linking more clearly the individual operator's performance with the group operating results. The activation of a new conception of shop-floor leadership was forced in part by the changes in control procedures (a mainly "technical" change) that made it possible for supervisors to become concerned with larger planning and coordination problems and then required them to do so by the sheer pressure of time. The use of group discussion and planning in connection with changes in floor layout and production planning not only aided the technical changes but themselves reinforced the effort to introduce group processes as a normal way of shop coordination.

In a similar fashion, the changes in the technology of scheduling, of information generation and flow, of work-load balancing, allocation of staff services, and the like, nearly all had features that aided social changes of the desired kinds and in turn were made possible by coordinated efforts to change individual behavior and to change the relations among the Weldon people. Where this linkage was lacking or weak, the change program faltered.

Leverage and Progression

The intent of organizational change presents immediately the problem of an entry point for the change program. Lippitt,

Watson, and Westley[9] refer to this as the "leverage point," defined in terms of accessibility (i.e., openness to influence) and linkage (lines of progress from the leverage point to the part of the social system that is the ultimate change target). In the Weldon case, the leverage point in the plant was the top management group, composed of people clearly having both the responsibility and the authority to act, and a group easily accessible to the influence of the new owners. This may not at first seem like a choice at all, for it is a platitude to think of "starting at the top." This should be viewed, however, as a deliberate choice, for alternatives are often available, and many change programs do have their leverage point elsewhere, at lower or middle ranks, or in some single functional unit.

The progression linkage within the Weldon organization followed, for the most part, the existing formal structure of the organization. This is seen most clearly in the choice of "family groups" for the management and supervisory training sessions, and the use of supervisors and assistant supervisors in such activities as the problem-solving session with operators and earnings development work with operators. The family group laboratory training sessions were held in sequence with groups from the top down and in close temporal proximity. All of the various programs involved the relevant line and staff people either as coplanners or, more often, as active participants in their normal role relationships, with a view toward their dual function of accomplishing the immediate program ends while at the same time developing the roles and competencies of the Weldon people. In these ways, the Weldon program avoided unnecessary confusion of the formal structure of the organization and contributed to the clarity of roles and responsibilities within the organization. The chief exceptions to this were in the presence of temporary consultants and the personal intervention of the new owners and their representatives; they took care to minimize their disruption of the organizational linkages by involving the relevant Weldon

---

[9] R. Lippitt, J. Watson, and B. Westley, *The Dynamics of Planned Change*, New York, Harcourt, Brace, 1958.

people, to the extent thought possible, in their normal roles. The leverage point and the change progression linkages remained, after the end of the program, as intact features of the Weldon organization.

Resources for Change

It is a common failing in organizational change and development programs that the resources allocated are small while the task is large. Weldon avoided this error: Relatively large resources were put to work, and these resources included not only money as needed, but also the diversion of internal staff to change efforts, the introduction of specialized and supplemental consulting staff from outside, additions to the permanent Weldon staff, and the application of a significant amount of talent and time by the new owners and their representatives. One reason for the success of the Weldon program, we believe, lies in the sheer amount and variety of resources put to work. The direct dollar costs of the change efforts on the human organization side were of about the same magnitude as the direct dollar cost of physical plant improvement; this is a relationship that may have general applicability in labor-intensive industries, although perhaps not in capital-intensive industries.

Aside from the scale of investment of change resources, it is to be noted that the main input was in the form of ideas about what changes were needed and how they might be achieved. These ideas came from outside of the Weldon organization. Mann and Hoffman,[10] among others, have commented upon the conditions that optimize the chances for an organization to undertake change, asserting that an organization is "ready" for change when it has (1) a supportive management history (2) good management-union relations, (3) a sizable fund of mutual trust and goodwill, and (4) members (employees) who are satisfied with the organization.

---

[10] F. C. Mann and L. R. Hoffman, *Automation and the Worker: A Study of Social Change in Power Plants*, New York, Holt, Rinehart and Winston, 1960.

We may point out, however, that a company enjoying the characteristics just mentioned is unlikely to find itself in need of drastic change, since its internal posture toward the world is one of flexibility and adaptability. Like water seeking its own level, the various functional units and subsystems of an organization tend to be of similar quality: It is likely that a technically antiquated organization will also demonstrate antiquity in its social system; it is likely also that an organization interested in scientific, technical advancement will, sooner or later, come to organizational advancement as well.

A frequent change problem, therefore, is not one of improving the excellent, but of making the passable better, or of rescuing the destitute. In the Weldon case, the basic problem was how to create radical change in a declining organization when (1) management's history was anything but supportive, (2) union-management relations have been hostile, (3) there was little trust and a lot of ill will, and (4) employees were generally dissatisfied and suspicious. Basic technical and organizational reforms ordinarily cannot, in such a situation, wait for the slow process of self-generated social change. Instead, we must see whether it is possible, as it was in the present study, to redirect the accommodative processes of the organization away from a rigid fixation on ideas that would doom it to failure, and toward ideas that offer a chance for survival and success. We think that in such a situation, external resources are often required. It is likely that intervention by the new owners, and some coercive steps by them, made the Weldon success possible. The program was planned and carried out, however, with an awareness of the costs associated with coercion, and with a willingness to accept these costs if they seemed unavoidable. Some of the demands placed upon Weldon managers by the new owners were, to put it mildly, pre-emptory and compelling, but always coupled with apparently limitless moral support and practical aid. Among operators, the enforcement of absence and termination rules was uncompromising, but applied only after liberal expenditure of encouragement and personal aid to the individual operator.

Comparison of Manufacturing and Merchandising

The preceding pages have referred to the Weldon manufacturing plant organization. The situation in the merchandising division was rather different, and the organizational change events were different.[11] It is useful to compare the developmental histories of the two divisions in terms of the factors in organizational change we have mentioned in the preceding pages.

The chief fact to be accounted for is that while in the plant the change program was brought about by altering individual behavior, technology, and social processes, in merchandising the change in performance was brought about by "revolution"—i.e., by replacing a large proportion of the key people. In the plant, although one other person left, the only significant change of managerial staff was the gradual withdrawal of the former owner-director; his personal intervention in plant affairs had already diminished before the change program began, and he soon, at the age of 70, withdrew to a consulting role and then retired entirely. His departure was gradual and was little noticed by most people in the plant. In merchandising, on the other hand, five of the six top people departed. The improvement of merchandising performance was brought about by the five new men and the one carry-over man.

The Weldon merchandising organization did not offer, as the plant did, a leverage point for organizational change. The former owner-director, who was continued on as the top executive, was not receptive to ideas of change. Over the years, personal dependency upon him had been fostered, and several persons with ability and initiative had already left. There did not appear to be any person or unit in the merchandising organization where there was the technical ability, the authority, or the organizational linkages that offered an entry for a change program.

The available resources for change were limited. The new

---

[11] The description of the merchandising division appears in Chapters 1 and 9.

owners, and their representatives, while expert in manufacturing processes, were not equally so in the kind of marketing activity on which Weldon's business was based. The expertness within the Weldon merchandising organization could not be brought effectively to bear on the problems. It seemed unlikely that outside consultants, even if they could be found, would be able to work effectively within the existing organizational system.

In the manufacturing plant, there was early assent, although perhaps superficially, to the general goals and nature of the change program—an assent including the plant manager, his staff, and his supervisors. In the merchandising division, in contrast, the suggestions for modification of goals and of organizational processes had the effect initially of heightening the "loyalty" of staff to their director in resisting change, and later, when the training sessions opened channels of communication among this staff, the authoritarian structure crumbled, leaving the director (the only person of authority) without support and still unwilling to be influenced by his own staff. The strain of old loyalties (two of the staff were relatives of the director) coupled with dissolution of the only authority structure they knew, proved too much. In addition, the staff were aware of the intricate strategies employed by their director in maintaining the firm's façade prior to disposing of it, and felt unable to deal with the situation. Only one could be persuaded to stay on.

In sum, the change program within the merchandising division never really got under way, for want of a point of leverage, for want of consent—or the hope of consent—to changed goals, for want of internal resources for change and because of inability to bring to bear external resources.

Some Uncertainties

Any analysis of a complex change process is likely to raise some new issues as well as to clarify some old ones, and that is true in this case.

We have argued that technical and social systems are interdependent, that technical changes can be a vehicle for advancing desired changes in the social organization, and vice versa. But we have not, in this case, been able to demonstrate such interdependence clearly, nor have we been able to assess the relative effect of technical and social changes on the net outcome of organizational performance. It seems likely that some neater, and better-controlled, experimental procedures will be necessary to clarify issues surrounding the interaction, or mutual dependence, of concurrent changes in a sociotechnical system.

The data show that the motives and performance of employees at the Weldon plant changed. Operators were observed to work harder, and they reported that they felt themselves to be working harder. Supervisors were observed, and reported themselves, to change from a self-protective to a collaborative rule for their own behavior. Did the change in motives "cause" the change in work performance? Did the improved performance arise from improved work arrangements and in turn give rise to alteration of individual motives? We suspect there is in this process a "snowball" effect, such that motivational changes and performance changes enhance one another, that increased motivation toward work effort is not likely to arise unless the efforts can show a visible improvement in work outcome, that improvement in work arrangements is unlikely to improve results unless there are some initial voluntary attempts, from internal, personal sources, to try out the motive-satisfying properties of the new work arrangements. Our case does not clarify at all the questions surrounding the initiation of concurrent changes in motivation and work performance.

The Weldon change program had some clear elements of coercive pressure, even though based upon a philosophy of management that views coercion as being relatively costly and ineffective. The paradox of using coercion to break up and rebuild an existing coercive social system is a common one, and one that forces a concern about the conditions under which a manager should use directive, as compared with consultative or participative, strategies. The data show clearly that the Weldon plant was changed from a mainly coercive to a mainly voluntaristic social system, but does not reveal much about the problem of optimizing or balancing the two themes in the case of contractual organizations (such as a factory) of large size that must accommodate to changing environmental conditions.

The survey data in the Weldon plant were singularly difficult to interpret and to correlate with behavioral changes. For example, while observers and top-level participants agreed that there was a marked change in the power structure at Weldon, the employees, in their survey, reported little or no change. The effort and output of the operators changed sharply, but on the attitude questionnaires they showed only a modest shift toward more positive attitudes regarding the company and the work. The operator's views regarding their supervisory leadership were obscured by a concurrent change in the source of this leadership in a manner that discouraged proof of a linkage between behavioral change and changes in supervisory practices. We think it is not appropriate to conclude that survey data—attitude questionnaires—are irrelevant or misleading in the analysis of organizational conditions and changes; it is more plausible to conclude that attitudes are very stable and slow to change, in comparison with work behavior, which may be more volatile and easier to change. The Weldon case thus highlights the uncertainty about the relative pace of changes of different kinds in a social system.

Will the changes at Weldon last? The only evidence we have at the present time is that the change from a predominantly "authoritative" to a dominantly "consultative" type of management organization persisted for at least two years, in the view of the managers and supervisors involved. Surely there exist forces toward a reversion to the old Weldon form of organizational life; it remains an uncertainty whether they will or will not win out over the new forces toward consolidation of change and toward further change of intended kinds.

Pointers for Managers

For managers, the main lessons of the Weldon case can be summarized in a few points:

Acquisitions, traditionally based mainly on economic and market considerations, need to be based as well upon a consideration of the state of the human organization of both the acquiring and the acquired firms. Failure to estimate the viability of an organization, failure to take steps to preserve the human resources of the acquired firm, failure to estimate correctly the heavy demands upon the material and technical (including sociotechnical) resources, are frequent causes of acquisition failures. The means, and the legal and ethical considerations, in assessing the organizational characteristics of a firm for acquisition, have not been developed, but must surely be explored, as these considerations are vital ones.

An organizational system can be radically changed and improved in a relatively short time, provided there is a coherent guiding philosophy, ample resources for change efforts, and some coordination between technical changes and the associated social changes.

The managerial philosophy adopted by Harwood in the Weldon case, while not the only one available and not necessarily the best, has much merit and deserves serious consideration, not only for acquired firms but as well for firms seeking to improve their own performance.

A good deal of time and effort can be saved by improved coordination and conceptual consolidation between the several management-related sciences and technologies. The traditional separation—even antagonism—between the professions concerned with technologies and work systems, and those concerned with human and organizational behavior, is clearly no longer to be tolerated. It is the job of managers to join them in practice.

17

THE HUMAN ORGANIZATION

Alfred J. Marrow

IN RECENT YEARS, industry has been in an explosive expansion. Large domestic corporations have become global enterprises, small regional companies have become national firms. This has happened not only in key industries such as electronics, chemicals, and aircraft, which require advanced technology, but in all others.

As our economy continues to expand, organizations grow larger, more complex, and more difficult to manage with traditional practices. Budgeting, marketing, long-range planning, and other company functions require greater collaboration and feelings of interdependence among the members of an organization. This must be accomplished at a time when specialties are diverging, geographical distances growing, internal fragmentation increasing, and self-serving parochial interests mounting.

Major alterations in managerial practices are necessary to disperse power and increase efficiency, to induce greater intergroup cooperation and teamwork, and to raise motivation. More than ever, we are in an age when growth and survival cannot be taken for granted, an age when no organization can assume everything will remain the same, or that the same methods, procedures, and principles will be successful in the future—as in the past. An organization that stands still cannot outlive its rivals in a situation where competition has become worldwide even for the local factory or machine shop.

Only the "fittest" will survive in these constantly changing times, and this requires the capacity to learn, to innovate, to expand, and to alter traditions of business life that have remained unaltered for generations. But growth is not continuous at various times; rather, it responds to varying conditions. New tools, techniques, and knowledge are creating new situations and realities. All produce alterations in the human environment, provoking hostile human reactions. Organizations must respond by transforming themselves and their structures to keep pace with what is taking place.

The future belongs to those leaders of organizations who can demonstrate the necessary managerial skill and imagination to cope with the enormous changes around them. All organizations in these changing times (as contrasted with *Modern Times* of the 1920s) are confronted by the challenges of changing their structures, their patterns of management, and their leadership styles, if they are to function more effectively and attain their objectives. The days of the soulless corporation, the heartless capitalist, or the robber baron are gone. Their place has been taken by the enlightened management concerned with human behavior and social relationships —as well as technology and production.

The incredible speed of technological advances, the pace of social developments, the effect of new political policies, the pressures of competition all make the shift to new methods the overriding element in growth and survival. Concern for human development may decide the future of many currently successful organizations in the next decade. The importance of human factors is underlined in a report by the Brookings Institution on the 100 leading American companies in 1909. Only 36 remained among the top group in 1948. Despite financial strength, established reputations, and technical know-how, 64 lost their top positions because they failed to meet the needs of the people they dealt with—as employees, customers, or consumers. The Brookings Institution predicts similar patterns of failure in the next forty years.

The present level of productivity in American companies, which authorities estimate as using effectively only 50 per cent of the human potential, also reflects the human problem. The task is clear-cut: to discover how people can be motivated to perform at their best. To bring this about, managers must come to terms with dramatic changes in the social environment.

The work force itself has changed. The people in it constitute the best educated generation in history, a prideful contrast with earlier generations. At the beginning of the century, only 6 per cent of all young people graduated from high school, and this was reflected in the educational level of people entering industry. Today, while educational levels are rising, the requirements rise as well. Dropouts of partially educated students from their schools are a matter of national concern. Universal college-level education is forecast in the next decade for all who are capable of benefiting from it.

At one time, the educational gap between rank-and-file workers and company executives was wide and deep. This is no longer true and the gap will become less marked in the years ahead. It could usually be assumed in the past that the supervisors or managers were the most broadly skilled or technically knowledgeable persons in the enterprise. The assumption is no longer safe. It is now common that employees are more technically skilled than their supervisors. Even at the highest management levels, it is no longer unusual for a staff of Ph.D.'s in physics to be directed and coordinated by a company president who has had only an elementary college science course. But this is no handicap, for a manager's specialty is management, not science.

In the past, wide unemployment, economic disparities, and the unequal balance of power between manager and managed kept unrest beneath the surface. But the modern-minded, well-educated people now entering industry are the opposites of their counterparts fifty years ago. They do not hesitate to express their antagonism openly. They complain quickly if they feel the enterprise is overcontrolled and overorganized. They are always ready to switch jobs. The notion of a career with one company is disappearing, and the term "bureaucracy" has become an epithet.

In the conduct of their activities, organizations are finding themselves the targets of a rebellion that is taking place in every sphere of contemporary life: industry, community, church, colleges. Everywhere, there are hostile human reactions to practices that coerce and dominate, that demand dependency, or that operate by bureaucratic rules that create feelings of humiliation because of forced helplessness. These long-accepted authoritarian practices are now being openly challenged. We are witnessing their disappearance in the practices of many organizations—from the PTA to the Pentagon, the local laundry to the major steel producer—wherever the aim is to get the best out of human resources.

In the industrial setting, the consequences are evident in antagonistic relationships between individuals and between groups. There is distrust, indifference, and hostility between and within departments and at all levels. Among production workers it is reflected in loafing on the job, low performance, careless work practices, absenteeism, turnover and, ultimately, higher operating costs.

While this is a Monday-through-Sunday revolution affecting us all, nowhere is it more vividly expressed than in the younger generation. Young men and women have grown up in a period where independence from parental authority has been permitted, if not encouraged. They have been reared in homes where children have had more freedom to plan their own activities and make more important decisions than ever before in history. The experience has carried through school and has been expressed in many ways in both private and public life, sometimes destructively, but more often in positive ways. As the country's youth look ahead to adult life, they

demand jobs where they will be more than a number on a
punched card. They want what is labeled in their classrooms
as "self-actualization"—a demand that is now echoed throughout our society by all ages and socio-economic groups.

Meanwhile, the post-adolescent generation has become
particularly negative about careers in business and industry.
A recent study reported only 14 per cent of the graduates of
a leading university were planning business careers, compared
with 39 per cent five years earlier and 70 per cent in 1928.
"Business is for the birds," was the reaction on the Ivy League
campuses. Ominously, Harvard's placement director reports
that it is the brighter students who avoid business.

It is not the products of American industry that are in
disfavor. On the contrary, these are highly admired. It is
authoritarian managerial practices that are sharply criticized.
People in many organizations still feel that management per-
ceives them mechanically and point as evidence to misleading
analogies. They react with outrage to being viewed as "cogs"
in a "smooth-running machine," squares on a blueprint, or as
units in a "military" system characterized by chain of command, line and staff, rank and file.

Today, executives acknowledge the increasing importance
of changing the relationship of internal social environment.
This requires equal concern for the human as for the technical needs of the enterprise and a search for better ways of
integrating individual needs with organizational goals.

Such concern about human collaboration actually is rooted
in the American tradition of cooperative effort. What the
famous Frenchman Alexis de Tocqueville saw and wrote
about America more than one hundred years ago corresponds
to what we wish we could report today: "In no country in the
world has the principle of association been more successfully
used or applied to a great multitude of objects than in
America." Tocqueville attributed the strength and promise of
America to the people's capacity to work well together and to
solve their problems collectively. The pioneers were quick to
join hands, to work together, and to organize town meetings

to discuss common problems. They encouraged all to participate, and they succeeded by helping one another, advancing together to conquer new frontiers.

Today the greatest challenge confronting a conscientious executive has become the collaboration of people, particularly his managerial staff. He must turn his staff into an effective team of men who pull for the company, collaboratively but in their individual ways, instead of being "every man for himself." Moreover, as the company grows, new people mean more problems of coordination, communications, and motivation. It is more true than ever that productivity and performance in an organization depend more on the management of men than on the mere handling of machines.

The implications for modern organizations are inescapable, and most practitioners know that in our society they can no longer remain indifferent to the way people feel about their jobs, their supervisor, and their organization. If company policies and practices undermine the employee's feelings of pride and self-esteem, he will leave.

Because a job in our society is for the typical adult the center of his life, he wants to give more than his time and get more than his pay. He wants to do some thinking for himself, to make some decisions, to feel respected and trusted. Unfortunately, the responses to this demand have usually been out of step with what is currently known about human behavior. Too many companies are still influenced by outmoded notions about authority, obedience, and the prepotency of economic needs. To solve the troubles that result, too many managers try push-button panaceas. They fall back on old stereotypes about human nature: People are instinctively lazy, avoid decisions or make bad ones, shun responsibility, have no initiative, and must be closely supervised. Therefore, these organizations are run with controls based on distrust, overlapping layers of supervision, excessive records and reports, and bargaining on some matters that could be resolved more favorably to all if approached as a joint problem rather than as a competition.

In such organizations, there is little or no participation by workers in planning, goal-setting, or decision-making. An employee who earns his living in this kind of company finds that he lives in a democracy—except in the place where he works. The abrasive contrast between democracy in the home and the community and autocracy in the organization is responsible for much of the deep-seated resentment that creates tension and often explodes into open conflict.

It is our belief that the democratic manager—who encourages participative methods—will succeed best in the face of the changes that surround American organizations. Such a managerial process can be used equally by ambassador, university president, director of medical research, or the head of a profit-making enterprise. Good management is as necessary for the successful operation of a nonprofit organization or governmental agency as for a profit-making industrial corporation.

Unfortunately, our language is limited in words to describe the different types of leadership. The English language uses the word "leader" to denote persons who are dictators just as it does persons who lead by election. Thus Hitler and Abraham Lincoln are "leaders." But obviously the two types are far apart and must be distinguished. Similarly in community life, "leader" is commonly associated with Boy Scouts and jazz bands. In industry we fall back on special terms of "manager," "boss," "employer," "executive." Basically, the manager is a leader who has the central responsibility for the effective performance and well being of the human resources of the organization—as well as for the technological and economic components of his total enterprise system.

But leadership must be shared. Members of top management frequently overlook the importance of providing subordinates with a proportionate share of achievement satisfactions, yet always resist limits on their own freedom of decision. Managers insist, with justification, on power, appropriate amounts of recognition, and the opportunity to express opinions freely; they fail to see that the same needs exist in some degree in all others as well. Whether we call it self-respect, status, or self-esteem, such recognition is basic to the well being and performance of everyone in a company. When these needs are not satisfied, restlessness, quarrels, and conflict can result.

For any man on the job, the underlying reality is that the work he does, quite apart from economic rewards, is a central and focal point of his social and psychological existence. It helps him define who he is and what he is doing with his life. His relationships with others in the work environment affect his performance and influence his well being—on and off the job.

In any society a man works for bread alone, when he has no bread. Once primary needs for food and shelter are met, other needs, mostly psychological, become predominant and insistent. All human beings have a hierarchy of needs, and as the most urgent one is satisfied, others develop greater urgency. Hence, satisfactions, once gained, are taken for granted, and higher needs must be met to avoid dissatisfaction. The harassed manager who tries to satisfy his employees' apparently insatiable "psychic" demands may conclude, "Give them an inch and they want a mile." Can they ever be fully provided? Probably not. For the appetite increases with the eating when the appetite is for psychic income. Physical hungers can quickly be satisfied by food, water, warmth, or coolness every time they arise. Not so with psychological hungers.

While the friction created by the conflict between individual needs and organizational goals can never be eliminated, the friction can be minimized and the conflict managed. This is recognized more commonly by professional managers than by owner-managers. However, more companies of both kinds are seeking new managerial methods to help overcome the problems created by frustrations in the work environment. While *no* one management pattern can be recommended as ideal for every type of organization, it is certainly clear that superior results could be achieved in all organizations if there were more trust and openness, more sensitivity to the needs of others, more opportunities to build self-confidence and feelings of importance, more democracy in the organizational system.

Inevitably, the manager's focus has shifted to the interdependence of human and technological factors. He is confronted with a complex human network that calls for a new approach. He can no longer coerce—instead he must co-act with employees if they are to improve performances. His own competence depends upon a deeper self-knowledge and a clearer understanding of others if he is to gain their cooperation and to succeed in fusing business practices with human motivation. The philosopher Horace Kallen has suggested that a person's mind is constituted by *what* he minds, and with what satisfaction he minds it. Just as the terms musical mind, mathematical mind, or legal mind are used, so should the term managerial mind be applied to those who master the ideals, values, and skills of good leadership in organizations.

In the past this mastery has been pursued separately by the social scientist studying behavior in his laboratory and by the professional manager observing behavior in his organization. As a result, the practitioners have acquired valuable on-the-job experience, and the behavioral scientists have developed some highly refined theories.

Because of this separation, practitioners faced with the task of managing complex changes in their firms have had to act with primitive resources—with all the risks involved. Their success as leaders in maintaining cooperation and harmonious relationships illustrates a type of learning in the school of experience well described by Conant:

> Advances . . . were made without any very direct benefit of science. The ancient method of "let's-try-it-and-see" type of reasoning in solving immediate practical problems has led over the centuries to amazing results.[1]

In recent years, the separation has ended. Now there is an active collaboration between the practitioner and the theoretician, the manager and the behavioral scientist. The practi-

---

[1] James Bryant Conant (ed.), *Harvard Case Histories in Experimental Science*, Cambridge, Mass., Harvard University Press, 1957.

tioner's experience has been integrated with the theoretician's systematic concepts. Together, they amply fulfill Kurt Lewin's maxim that "nothing is so practical as a good theory." The application can revolutionalize organizational behavior and practices.

Index